BECAUSE GOD IS REAL

PETER J. KREEFT

Because God Is Real

Sixteen Questions,
One Answer

How to
"be ready to give a reason
for the hope that is in you"
— 1 Peter 3:15

IGNATIUS PRESS　　SAN FRANCISCO

Cover photograph © by Brian Adducci

Cover design by Riz Boncan Marsella

© 2008 Ignatius Press, San Francisco
All rights reserved
ISBN 978-1-58617-200-8
Library of Congress Control Number 2007927187
Printed in the United States of America ∞

Contents

Introduction

What is this book good for? What is it about?

This book is worthless unless it helps you answer three questions about yourself:

1. Who am I?
2. Where did I come from?
3. Where am I going?

1. All our lives, we keep discovering who we are. None of us comes to the end of that road in this life. None of us completely knows who we are, once we stop fooling ourselves.

You are a one-and-only individual that nobody could ever replace. Nobody who ever lived in the past was exactly like you, and no one who will ever live in the future will be exactly like you. You have a special job to do in this world that no one else can ever do. Each day of your life, you find out a little more about what that job is.

But you also share the same human nature with all other human beings. Your task on earth is to be you, the one and only you; but it is also to be a human being, and that task is the same for all of us. You take different courses in school, but we all take a course called Life. Life's greatest tragedy is to pass all your courses but flunk Life.

No one but you and God knows what your individual job in life is. But the Catholic Church knows a lot about what your task is as a human being, because the Church is simply the mail carrier for the Gospel, or "good news", of Jesus Christ, who gave the human race the final, ultimate answer to the question of what we are doing here, why we exist, what is the meaning of life. This book is about that answer.

2. Who you are depends on where you came from. If you came from Mars, you are a Martian. If you came merely from apes, then you are merely an ape. And if God created you in His own image, then you are the King's kid, not King Kong's kid.

3. Your origin and your nature are the key to your destiny, your purpose in life. If you are only dust, then your destiny is only dust—"to dust you shall return"—for you are only a body, not an immortal soul. At the opposite extreme, if you are a god or goddess, born in Heaven and somehow lost on earth, then your destiny is to escape the earth and the mortal body and return home, like E.T. You don't belong here. The Christian answer is neither of these. You belong here because God created you and put you here, but you are a soul as well as a body, and your destiny is to grow in perfection of both body and soul, both here and in Heaven after death.

Our modern secular culture tells you the first answer: you are dust, you are a clever ape. Some New Age type religions tell you the second answer, that you are not an animal but an angel, a pure spirit. Christianity tells you a third answer. Which answer you believe makes a difference to everything in your life, because it's a different "you".

∼

This book is for three groups of readers. It's for Catholic Confirmation classes, for other catechism or religious education classes, and for those who simply choose to read the book for themselves.

It is also for all ages *after* Confirmation as well as before. Confirmation should be the *beginning* of an ever-maturing religious education, not the end. The Christian faith is not kid stuff.

This book is for both teenagers and adults. The most basic principle of writing a book for children of any age is this: If adults can't enjoy and use your book, don't write it. Don't ever patronize, pander, or pat the little kiddies on the head. Don't talk down to them—level with them.

I'm old. I'm not going to pretend I'm "into" the current culture. Anyway, ten or twenty years from now, the current "in" culture will be just as "out of it", just as outdated, as the culture that was "in" when I was a kid.

So I decided to write an adult book that kids could understand too, instead of a kids' book. Your parents should read it as well as you.

～

Most textbooks are dull as dishwater, in any subject, even religion. Students who have to read them aren't usually very interested in what they say; they just try to remember enough to please their teacher or pass their test. They memorize what's in the book instead of understanding it.

I think that's a ridiculous waste of energy. For one thing, memorizing anything takes ten times more time than understanding it. For another thing, memorizing is always duller than understanding. That's true if the thing to be understood is something dull. And it's even more true when the thing to be understood is something exciting, like a murder mystery.

Well, the Church's Gospel, or "good news", is as exciting as a murder mystery. For at its heart there *is* a murder: the murder of God two thousand years ago in Jerusalem. And this God is the greatest of mysteries: who He is and why He put us here and why He came here and what His plans are for us. And all the rest of the story stems from that. The story is literally a matter of life or death—eternal life or death. If a book about that story isn't interesting, then that has to be the fault of the book, not the fault of the story.

A book is like a letter from one author to many readers. The many readers differ in sex, age, race, beliefs, education, and interests. But the readers do not differ in one thing: humanity. Human nature is the same in men and women, in adults and children, in different races, in different cultures. So I write this to all of you as one human being to another. It doesn't matter that I'm an old white male Dutch college professor and surfer and that you may be a young black female Jamaican high school student and dancer. We're both human; we're both in the same boat. We're different animals, but we're both on Noah's ark.

One other thing: I write not for groups or classes of people but for individuals. When you read this book, please don't think, "I'm only one out of a thousand people reading this book, so I have only one one-thousandth of the responsibility for understanding it and thinking about it." Think instead: "I have 100 percent of the responsibility. This is a private conversation. This book is a letter from the author to me alone." That's not a lie or a "let's pretend." That's the truth. Because you *are* alone now, reading this, just as I am alone now, writing it.

Actually, I have to correct that. We're never alone, because God is real. There's three of us here, not two. And that's the central point of this whole book.

~

Most of the old catechisms from before the 1960s had a question-and-answer format. For instance, the famous old Baltimore Catechism started this way:

1. *Who made you?*
   God made me.
2. *Why did God make you?*
   God made me to know Him, to love Him, and to serve Him in this world and to be happy with Him forever in the next.

God made me to know Him, to love Him, and to serve Him in this world and to be happy with Him forever in the next.

That format was clear, sharp, short, and simple. And there's nothing wrong with that. You can put deep and profound stuff into short and simple sentences. The two questions above are an example of that. Nearly all American Catholics before the sixties learned the Baltimore Catechism, and most of them still remember those first two questions, because they are both simple *and* profound.

Another good thing about the old format was that it was a dialogue, questions and answers, rather than a straight lecture. If you're like me, you get bored with most lectures, and the question-and-answer session after a lecture is always more interesting than the lecture.

But there were two things wrong with the old format. First, students were often expected *to memorize* it instead of *to under-*

stand it. And second, it was too simple and pat. It often failed to communicate the sense of depth, greatness, wonder, and mystery that is an essential dimension of anything real. The Catholic faith is not a set of neat little man-made ideas; it is the Gospel, the "good news", the amazing news about what God has done in our world and is doing in our lives.

I

Why are questions good?

1. Which questions are we talking about?

Our sixteen questions are no ordinary questions, like "What's on TV tonight?" or "Who is the president of France?" They are sixteen of the most important questions you can ask, like "Why do I exist?" and "Why must we die?" and "Why aren't we happy?"

2. What makes a question important?

"How much is 2,222,222 divided by 3.3?" is not an important question. "How much does he love me?" is an important question. "Who wrote *Our Town*?" is not an important question. "Is that our town that's on fire?" is an important question. "What will happen to the sun when it dies?" is not an important question (though it is an interesting one). "What will happen to me when I die?" is an important question.

What makes a question important? Important questions are questions that concern your whole being, that make a difference to your whole life.

Religious questions make a difference to your whole life. Answering them one way or the other makes your whole life radically different.

Here is an example: Is it possible for Jesus to be totally human and totally divine at the same time? This may not seem like an important question, but it is. Here's why.

If it's not possible for Jesus to be both fully divine and fully human, then either (a) Jesus is only the perfect human being but not God, or else (b) He's only God but not a real human being.

a. If He's only a human being, then He can't forgive our sins. He can't be our Savior from sin. And He can't rise from the dead or raise us up from the dead. And He can't unite us to God and take us to Heaven. For no merely human being can do any of that.

b. If He's not fully human, if His human nature was only an appearance, like a movie or a dream, or "virtual reality", then He didn't really grow or tire or feel pain and frustration like us, so He can't really understand our pains and weaknesses. God was never a human baby. God never had a mother. God was never a teenager. God never had to learn a trade like carpentry. God never got hungry and tired and lonely and angry and frustrated. God never suffered and died.

If either of these two "heresies" is true—if Jesus is not fully divine or if Jesus is not fully human—then we have no hope of Heaven. And that's as big a difference to our lives as anything can possibly be.

Take one more example of an important question that seems unimportant at first: What is the sacrament of ordination to the priesthood?

This question does not seem to be very interesting or important at all unless you are thinking of becoming a priest. But if the sacrament of ordination is not what the Church says it is, if it doesn't give the priest the real power to forgive sins in the confessional and the real power to consecrate the bread and wine and change them into the Body and Blood of Christ in the Eucharist, then when you go to confession the priest has no power to forgive your sins, and when you go to Mass you do not really receive Jesus Christ into your body, because the priest had no power to change bread and wine into Christ.

You see, the question makes a great difference to your whole life after all. For the difference between forgiven sins and unforgiven sins is a gigantic difference, and the difference between a little wafer of bread and Jesus Christ is an infinite difference.

Religious questions are important because they make a difference.

3. *Why are questions precious?*

First, because they're human.

It's human to question. All human beings ask questions. And *only* human beings ask questions. God doesn't have to ask questions because He knows everything. Angels don't ask questions the way we do because they know by a kind of mental telepathy with each other and with God. And animals don't ask questions because they don't have the language (although some do have the curiosity, like cats, dogs, and monkeys).

Second, questions are precious because they are the very best way to learn. Questioning means that your mind is hungry. If your body isn't hungry, you won't eat, and if you don't eat, you won't grow. If your mind is not hungry—if you don't have wonder and the desire to know—then you won't ask ques-

tions, and if you don't ask questions, you won't find truth—
and that means that your mind and soul and spirit won't grow.
Truth is your mind's food.

The more passionately you care about the question, the
more truth you will find. As Jesus said, "Seek, and you will
find" (Mt 7:7). There is nothing more meaningless than an
answer to a question that you're not asking and don't care
about.

Third, God wants you to ask questions. He designed you
that way. Jesus never discouraged questions. His disciples asked
some really stupid ones. Asking stupid questions is a very good
way to learn!

4. Should we question our faith?

Yes!—if the questioning is sincere and honest and motivated
by your wanting to know the truth and not by your wanting to
just play games or show off. Saint Paul says, "Test everything;
hold fast to what is good" (1 Thess 5:21). How can you know
what is good unless you first test it, unless you first question
it? The more deeply and honestly you question, the more you
will appreciate the answers you find.

But if you don't really like answers but only questions, then
you are not really honest in asking questions. To ask a question
is to say, "I want the answer!" Preferring questions to answers
is like preferring hunger to food. As G. K. Chesterton said,
an open mind is like an open mouth: it's open so that it can
chomp down on something solid.

5. *There are sixteen questions in this book, and each of them contains ten other questions. That's 16 × 10 = 160 questions. Isn't that too many?*

No. It's far too few. For this is important stuff. This is real!

6. *What if I'm not an intellectual? What if I'm not "into" ideas? Not everybody likes questions as much as philosophers and college professors, you know.*

Three answers:

  a. You don't have to be an intellectual to wonder. You just have to be a human being. You don't have to have a high IQ to appreciate questions. You just have to have a human mind. And we each have one of those.
  b. These aren't questions about *ideas*, but questions about real things, like God and death and the difference between good and evil.
  c. These questions are more than just questions. They are a *quest*. They invite you to a personal journey of discovery. You will succeed in this quest not merely by being intelligent but above all by having two even more important things than intelligence: honesty and courage.

7. *When you speak of questions and answers, do you mean to assume that there's objective truth out there, the same for everybody, and that if you disagree with that truth, your opinion is not just different but wrong? Do you mean to say that religion is like science that way? That what's true for you also must*

be true for me, because religion is about what is simply and absolutely true, whether we like it or not? Are you saying that God is just as objectively real as a rock, even though you can't see Him and even though you can't prove Him by the scientific method?

Yup.

You have to assume objective truth even to deny objective truth. Is it objectively true that there's no objective truth? Is it only "true for you" that there is only "truth-for-you"?

8. How can there be one and only one true answer to all sixteen of these questions?

Because there is only one real God.

You see, the greater the question is, the closer the answer gets to God, who is the greatest reality. And these sixteen questions are some of the biggest questions you can ask, and the only answer big enough to meet them is God.

9. What do you mean by "real" when you say God is real?

I mean that God really exists, that God is not a lie, a myth, a dream, or a fairy tale; that God is really "there", in objective reality; that He exists just as really as the sun exists or your mother exists.

Most people believe God exists. But among these people who believe God really exists, God is much more "real" to some of them than to others. And this shows us a second sense of the word "real". For some people, God is like the moon: He's *there*, but not *here*. He exists, but He's not really present to their lives. Once in a while they notice Him, as they notice the moon once in a while, but most of the time He makes no difference to them. Their lives would not change much if they stopped believing in Him.

But for other people, God is like their best friend or their mother: He makes a tremendous difference to everything. If these people were to stop believing in God, it would change everything for them. It would be like their parents dying. They would become cosmic orphans.

So that's a second meaning of "real": a thing is real if it not only really exists but also *makes a real difference to your life*. Let's call that "personally real".

There is a third way we use "real". A thing is real if it is authentic, genuine, not fake—like real money as distinct from counterfeit money. We say of someone that he is "real" and we say of another that he is fake, or phony. They're not trustworthy. You can't rely on them to keep their promises.

God is real in all three ways. First, He is there, He really exists, He is "objectively real". Second, He is present to us, to our lives. He makes a difference, He is "personally real". Third, He is true, He is totally authentic and reliable, He is the "real thing".

10. What do you mean by "God"?

Here is what all Christians—Roman Catholics and Eastern Orthodox and Anglicans and Protestants—mean by "God":

a. *An objectively real being.* God really exists.

b. *The Creator.* God created the entire universe. When we humans create things, like inventions or plays or symphonies, we always create them out of something that was already there.

The Wright Brothers created their first airplane out of metal and wood. Shakespeare created his play *Macbeth* out of words and out of older stories. Beethoven created his symphonies out of sounds. (Even when he became deaf, he heard the sounds in his mind.) But God created the universe out of nothing. There was nothing He needed to rely on. There was nothing there before the universe was created, except God.

c. *An all-powerful being.* Since God can create out of nothing, God must be "omnipotent", or all-powerful. He is *infinitely* powerful; in other words, there is no limit to His power. He can do anything. (Can He create a rock bigger than He can lift? No, because a rock bigger than infinite power can lift is not anything at all. It's like a really red ball that's not really red and not really a ball—it doesn't mean anything. God can create miracles but not meaninglessness.)

d. *A pure spirit, not matter.* Everything made of matter is limited in space, in time, and in power. But God is not limited.

Matter also can't know or love. Only spirit can. Knowing and loving are the two acts of spirit, the two things that only spirit can do.

God, angels, and human persons are spirits. God is infinite spirit without matter. Angels are finite spirits without matter. Human persons are finite spirits with matter, with material bodies.

e. *An all-knowing being.* Since God is spirit, and spirit knows, God knows. And since God's power is infinite, His power to know is also infinite. God knows everything. He is all-knowing, or "omniscient". He knows every hair on our head (Mt 10:30).

f. *An all-loving being.* God loves everything lovable, everything good. He loves every grain of sand and every blade of grass, and certainly every person. For He created them all; He loved them into existence. When we said that God created "out of nothing", we meant "out of no matter" but not "out of no motive". His motive was love.

g. *A being with a will.* Since God loves us, He wills what is good for us. That is why He gave us commandments. They are the road to our good and our happiness.

h. *A Trinity of Persons.* "God is love" (1 Jn 4:8). God is not just one who loves; God is complete love itself. Complete love itself includes (1) a lover, (2) a beloved, and (3) the act of loving that flows between the lover and the beloved. In God, these are (1) the Father, (2) the Son, and (3) the Holy Spirit, one God in three divine Persons, who make up complete love.

This is the doctrine of the *Trinity*, the tri-unity of God. There is only one God, not three, but this one God *is* the three Persons, the Father, the Son, and the Holy Spirit. They are not three *parts* of God; all three are God totally. God can't be divided into parts.

The above paragraph is certainly the most difficult and mysterious paragraph in this entire book. Naturally! For the truth that this paragraph teaches is the most difficult and mysterious truth in all of human knowledge. We could never have discovered it ourselves; God had to reveal it to us. (The Bible is the story of God's gradual revelation of Himself to us.)

i. *A Person.* God the Father, God the Son, and God the Holy Spirit are all Persons. There is only one God, but this one God is three divine Persons. When God the Father revealed His own true name to Moses, in the burning bush (see Ex 3), He said, "I AM WHO I AM." "I" refers to a person. Only a person can say "I". We know three kinds of persons: divine, angelic, and human. God created us in His own image, and that means that we too, like God, can say "I", as no animal can.

j. *A being who revealed Himself.* Here is why God had to reveal Himself to us in order for us to know Him, why "divine revelation" was necessary.

When you want to get to know something less than yourself, you have to do most of the work. (A rock won't do anything except just sit there, and a tree won't do anything except grow, and even an animal will only move around, but it won't have a conversation with you.) When you want to get to know something equal to yourself, another human being, both of you have to be active and do the work of conversation. When you want to know God, who is infinitely greater than you, He has to take the initiative and reveal Himself. That's why there had to be divine revelation. Just as adults teach babies and babies don't teach adults, so God teaches us and we don't teach God.

This is also how we know that this answer to the question "What do you mean by 'God'?" is the true answer: because it is not our answer but God's. God revealed it, and God cannot lie; He can neither deceive nor be deceived.

k. Why did God reveal Himself? To establish a relationship with us. The word "religion" means, fundamentally, "relationship". True religion is a love-relationship with God.

l. How did God reveal Himself? The answer to that question is the story of the Bible, culminating in Christ and the Church that Christ established. We will explore more details of that revelation in later chapters of this book.

II

Why do I exist?

1. What is that question doing here, in this book? "Why do I exist?"—what a strange question! Not the kind of thing I expected to find in a catechism textbook about the Catholic religion. It sounds very abstract and vague and speculative.

If that's what you thought when you read the title of this chapter, I have to tell you that you were mistaken, in three ways.

First of all, it is not a strange question at all, but a very natural question. Everyone asks it, consciously or unconsciously, though not necessarily in those words.

Second, it is a religious question. It is a question to which all religions claim to have an answer.

Finally, it is not abstract but as concrete and particular as you are. It's about your life.

2. Why is my existence in question?

Because you didn't *have* to exist. If one little thing had happened differently to any of your ancestors, you would not exist. For instance, if your great-grandfather hadn't been surprised by the sound of a squirrel dropping a nut on a dry leaf in the park where he was sitting on a bench a hundred years ago, he wouldn't have turned his head around to see what the noise was, and he wouldn't have noticed the pretty girl on the bench over there, walked over and struck up a conversation with her, got to know her, and eventually married her—and you are part of the rest of that story.

So is it just luck that you exist? Just chance? Did you just happen, or are you designed? Are you an accident, or are you wanted? Are you just lost on a stage without any lines to speak, just making it all up as you go along, or are you part of a play, a plot, a plan, with an Author's mind behind it?

You can't get the answer to that question just from your feelings, because your feelings change from year to year, day to day, even minute to minute. Everyone at times feels lost and meaningless, and everyone at other times feels part of a meaningful story.

It makes all the difference in the world how you answer that question. It amounts to asking whether your life has real meaning or not.

We deeply want our lives to have a real meaning. But where does this real meaning come from? Why is there a real answer to the question "Why do I exist?"

Because God is real, that's why. Because you were willed into existence by an all-knowing, all-loving, and all-powerful God. *That's* why your life has meaning and purpose.

3. How can we know the true answer to this question about the meaning of our life? What must we know, to know who we are?

The secret of your identity is in the mind of your Creator and Designer. Therefore, to find the meaning of your life, you must know God. To find out who Macbeth is, you must ask Shakespeare. To find out who Gollum is, you must ask Tolkien. To find out who you are, you must ask God.

How do we know God? Through Christ. "No one has seen ever seen God; the only Son . . . has made him known" (Jn 1:18).

To know yourself adequately, you must know God. And to know God adequately, you must know Christ. Therefore, to know yourself adequately, you must know Christ. Christ reveals not just who God is but also who we are.

4. *When we ask why we exist, what do we seek?*

We seek our origin, our nature, and our destiny. There are actually three parts to this question: "Where did I come from?" and "What am I?" and "Where am I going?"

There are two radically different possible answers to this three-part question: the no-God answer and the God-answer. We exist either because of mere chance and accident or because of divine design; we exist either because of blind matter below us or because of conscious divine spirit above us.

The three questions (of origin, nature, and destiny) are closely connected. If our *origin* is only material, if we came only from mindless matter blindly bumping into more mindless matter and not from the Mind of God designing and creating our matter, then our *nature* is also only matter: we are only apes with bigger brains but no souls. If our parents were only big apes, we are only big apes. And then our *destiny*, our end, is only the destiny of all matter and animal life: death and decay. Period. End of story. That is the logical consequence of believing that there is no God. Death wins in the end.

But if our origin is from above, from God—if we are designed and created by an intelligent Spirit—then our nature can be also spiritual, made in the image of the God who is spirit. God may have used evolution to make our bodies out of previously existing animal species, but souls cannot evolve. God must create each soul afresh.

If that is true—if we exist because of God, if we are real because God is real—then the practical consequences are tremendously important. For then each one of us has intrinsic dignity. That means that we are not mere objects to be used by other objects. We are God's kids!

And then our destiny (the third connected question) is also spiritual: to live forever with God in Heaven. God is our first beginning and our last end, our ultimate origin and our ultimate destiny.

	RELIGIOUS VIEW OF MAN	NONRELIGIOUS VIEW OF MAN
ORIGIN:	God	mere matter
NATURE:	image of God, children of God	mere animal
DESTINY:	eternal life with God	mere death

5. *What do we mean when we say that God is our origin?*

We mean that He created us out of nothing. Genesis 2:7 tells us that He formed our bodies out of "dust from the ground" (possibly a symbolic image for previously existing matter), but He created our souls directly, out of nothing material.

The truth that we were created has enormous practical consequences for our lives. Because God is our Creator, we owe *everything* to Him, because we owe Him our very existence. Just as we owe Him thanks for the whole universe outside of us because we did not make it but it is a gift from Him, so we owe Him thanks for our very selves, body and soul, because we did not make that either. Our very existence is His gift.

We have rights over against each other, but not over against God. For God is not one finite part of the universe, as we are. He is outside the universe. (That does not mean He is in some space outside the universe but that He is more than the universe, He is transcendent to the universe.) God is not our equal. Our relation to God is not like the relation between Mark Antony and Brutus, two equal characters in the same Shakespearean play, *Julius Caesar*. Neither is it like the relation between Shakespeare and his wife, two equal persons in Elizabethan England. It is like the relation between Brutus and Shakespeare. It is the relation between a creature and his creator.

That is why we have rights over against each other but not over against God. Brutus has rights over against Mark Antony but not over against Shakespeare. Shakespeare's wife has rights over against Shakespeare but not over against God. God is not your equal. God is your God.

6. *What do we mean when we say God is our end or destiny? That sounds very vague and airy and abstract. Can you make it more concrete and down-to-earth and easier to understand?*

Yes.

Our end is happiness. When anything attains its end or destiny or purpose, it is happy. Fish are happy swimming, not running. Birds are happy flying, not swimming. Lions are happy running free, not in a cage. If we find out what our destiny and purpose are, we find out how to be happy. It's like people who are lost finding their way home (like E.T.). They're happier at home because that's where their destiny is, that's where they belong.

God designed us to be happy—truly, deeply, permanently happy. He designed us to be partially happy with the good things He created for us in this world, and totally happy only in Heaven with the infinite good, the only infinite good that exists, Himself. That is why, as Saint Augustine said, "Our hearts are restless until they rest in You": because "You have made us for Yourself." Your heart is like an infinitely large hole, and only God is big enough to fill it.

7. *How can God fill our hearts? When we say our destiny is union with God, what does that mean? How can we be united with God?*

It means two things: to be *like* God more and more in this world, and to be *with* God forever in Heaven.

To be *like* God means above all to love, because "God is love" (1 Jn 4:8). That's why loving makes us more deeply happy than anything else ever does and why refusing to love, being selfish, makes us deeply unhappy and lonely.

To be *with* God means what the saints call "spiritual marriage": to be in a close, personal, intimate love-relationship with God; to know Him even better than human friends or lovers can ever know each other. That is how Jesus defines the life of Heaven: "This is eternal life, that they know thee the only true God" (Jn 17:3). Not just to know *of* Him or to know *about* Him, but to know *Him*.

8. *So the meaning of life is . . . to be a saint?*

Exactly! But being a saint does not necessarily mean being someone unusual and famous, like Saint Francis of Assisi or

Mother Teresa. It means simply loving God with your whole heart and loving your neighbor as you love yourself (Mt 19:19).

This is *every* person's destiny. Most of us have a long, long way to go to reach it. But God cares about every one of His children, even the ones who are the slowest to learn to walk down the road of love, the only road that leads to Heaven. God cares about the smallest steps we take on this road, the tiniest choices to love. He is our Father, after all; that's why He is "easy to please and hard to satisfy", as C. S. Lewis' friend George MacDonald put it. God is pleased with the first little baby steps we take on this royal road of love, but He will not be satisfied until we are mature and whole and reach the end of the road.

That's one reason why the process of learning to love completely will be completed after death in Purgatory for most of us: because we're not finished yet. Although Baptism and faith have made us "justified" (or "saved", or "in a state of grace"), so that we can go to Heaven, we still need to do good works, the works of love, throughout our lives in order to grow into saints, in order to be "sanctified".

Meanwhile, life is a road to that end. Here is what life looks like from the perspective of that end, that destiny:

It is a serious thing to live in a world of possible gods and goddesses, to realize that the dullest person you meet may one day be something which, if you saw it now, you would be strongly tempted to worship; or else a horror and a corruption which you meet now only in a nightmare. All day long we are helping each other to one or the other of these two destinations. There are no ordinary people. You have never met a mere mortal. Nations, cultures, arts, civilizations, these are mortal, and their life is to ours as the life of a gnat. But it is immortals whom we work with, play with, marry, snub, or exploit: immortal horrors or everlasting splendors (C. S. Lewis, "The Weight of Glory").

9. *Why doesn't everybody believe that this is our purpose and destiny?*

Because some people think there *is* no real purpose or destiny to human life! They believe that only the things *we* make, like cars and watches, have design and purpose in them. We know what the purposes of these objects are because we designed them. (For instance, we know that the purpose of a car is transportation, and the purpose of a watch is to tell time.) But the things in nature, like trees and stars, were not designed by any human beings, so we do not know their purposes as we know the purposes of the things we design. So some people believe that there *are* no real purposes in the things in nature, but only in humanly designed artificial objects.

But one of the things in nature is human beings. They are not artificial objects! They are not artifacts like cars or watches. We did not design human nature; we only carry it on, by reproduction.

So the people who deny that human life has any real purpose argue this way:

> If only artifacts have purposes, while things in nature
>   do not;
> And if we are things in nature rather than artifacts;
> Then we have no real purpose.

So the answer to the question "What is the purpose of my existence?" is that there *is* no real purpose; we can imagine or make up any subjective purposes we want, but there is no objectively real purpose to human life. Life is purposeless, pointless, meaningless, in vain. "Vanity of vanities! All is vanity" (Eccl 1:2).

This is the worst philosophy in the world. For it denies us the things we need most: meaning and purpose; a reason to live, learn, grow, and endure.

Meaninglessness is unendurable. Even pain isn't as bad as meaninglessness. We can accept pains if they are meaningful: for instance, the pains of childbirth, or the pains of sacrificing for someone you love, or even the pains of martyrdom for a good cause. But we cannot accept meaninglessness. Even pleasures are not worthwhile if they are meaningless. (That's why a billionaire can choose to commit suicide.) And even pains are worthwhile if they are meaningful. (That's why a woman wants to give birth to a baby.)

The idea that objective things have no purpose is really atheism. For if God is real and if He created and designed everything, then *everything* has a purpose.

We can see some of the purposes of the things in nature. For instance, we can see that one of the purposes of stars is to enable us to think. For (a) if we did not breathe and bring oxygen to our brains, we could not think; and (b) if there were no green plants, we could not breathe, since their photosynthesis replaces carbon dioxide with oxygen; and (c) if there were no sun, there could be no green plants, for green plants need sunlight and heat; and (d) if there were no stars, there would be no sun, for the sun is a star. Therefore, if there were no stars, we could not think.

But many of the things in nature have designs and purposes that are not clear to us. They do not seem to be useful for us. (For instance, we wonder why God made so many mosquitoes.) So it takes a little faith, a little trust, to *believe* that everything has a purpose and that "all things work together for good to those who love God, who are called according to His purpose" (Rom 8:28), even though we do not *see* this. This is especially true of things that make us suffer. We do not always see how suffering has a good purpose.

But if the Creator is all-wise, all-good, and all-powerful, then the quotation above from Romans 8:28 must be true. If He is all-good, He wants what is best. If He is all-powerful, He is able to bring about what is best, in the end. And if He is all-wise, He knows what is best.

And since we are *not* all-wise, we do not know what is best in the long run. That is why we have to trust Him with all those mosquitoes and even with much worse things, like cancers. He knows how to bring greater goods out of great evils. That is what He did two thousand years ago on the Cross of Calvary when He brought about the greatest good for us, the greatest gift we have ever been given—salvation from sin and the ability to enter Heaven—through the greatest evil that ever happened, the torture and murder of Jesus Christ, the only perfect man who ever lived, the man who was God Himself.

10. We Christians believe this. Many people don't. Can we give them any reason to believe our religion's answer to the question "Why do I exist"?

The best reason we can give them is ourselves: our love and our joy. You can't argue with the happiness of a saint.

The greatest love, and the greatest joy, is mutual: it comes from both loving and being loved. The next-greatest joy comes from loving, even without being loved back. Even this second-best joy of loving without being loved back is greater and deeper than the third joy, the joy of being loved without loving. That is why saints are so happy: they are never in the third level of joy but always in the second or the first. (In fact, since they know God always loves them, you could say they are always in the first.)

That's why the prayer attributed to Saint Francis says

Lord, make me an instrument of Your peace. Where there is hatred, let me sow love; where there is injury, pardon; where there is doubt, faith; where there is despair, hope; where there is darkness, light; and where there is sadness, joy. O divine Master, may I always seek *not so much to be consoled as to console, to be understood as to understand, to be loved as to love. For it is in giving that we receive, it is in pardoning that we are pardoned, and it is in dying that we are born to eternal life.* Amen.

III

Why is faith reasonable?

1. What is "faith" and what is "reason"?

"Faith" means *believing*: believing either some *thing*, some idea (like "$E = mc^2$" or "The sun will rise tomorrow"), or some*one*, that is, trusting a person.

"Reason" means *knowing* something to be true with your mind. Especially, it means proving something to be true, giving good reasons.

Proving something is only one way of coming to know it. We are going to explore different ways of knowing God, and faith and reason are two of those ways.

We will prove that God is real in the next chapter. In this chapter, we will explore different ways of knowing God, especially the relation between faith (believing) and reason (proving).

2. What are the different ways of knowing? How do we know anything at all?

We have three ways of knowing anything. We could call them three "eyes". The first eye is in the physical body: it is the five senses (sight, hearing, touch, taste, and smell). The second eye is in the soul: it is the mind, the reason, the intellect. We often call this the "head", though it is not just the physical head.

A third eye is in the heart. This is not the *physical* heart, the organ in the center of the body that pumps the blood, but the power at the center of the *soul*. The heart does not see with the bodily eyes, nor does it reason and prove with the intellect, but it "just knows", or intuits, or "sees" with the inner eye, the eye of the heart. ("Heart" does not mean "sentiment" or "emotion" here but something deeper. It is a way of *knowing*, not just feeling.)

We use our senses to know material things, like stars and jars and cars. We use our minds (our heads) to know abstract truths like mathematics, logic, and scientific principles. We use our hearts (as well as our senses and our reason) to know people: ourselves and others. Sense-knowledge is the best way to know material things. Intellectual knowledge is the best way to know abstract truths. Heart-knowledge is the best way to know people.

We know people in all three ways. But the person who has only sense-knowledge of you, or only head-knowledge of you, does not know you as well as the person who has heart-knowledge of you, who knows you "by heart".

Now let's apply these three ways of knowing to God.

3. How do we know God?

We can know God with two of our three "eyes". He can be known with the head (by reason) and with the heart (by faith, hope, and love), but not with the senses.

God cannot be sensed because He does not have a material body. He does not have a material body because He is infinite. "Infinite" means "unlimited". Material bodies are limited, since they exist only in some places and not others and only at some times and not others. No material body exists everywhere and at every time. But God does.

Although He is not a *human* person, God is a Person (actually, three divine Persons), so He is known best as any person is known best: by the heart's experience, especially the experience of loving Him. That is the best way to know a human person too: by genuine, unselfish love. We all know that. Think about this: Which of these two friends of yours knows you better? Friend A, who is very intelligent but loves you and cares about you only a little, or friend B, who is less intelligent but who loves you and cares about you very, very much? Who knows you better, your teacher or your mother?

4. If we know God best by the heart, why do we need to prove God's existence with the reason?

Because some people do not believe He exists.

Human persons can be seen with the senses (the first eye), so we don't have to use the second eye, the eye of reason, to prove that human persons exist. But God cannot be sensed (by the first eye). So we need to prove His existence (with the second eye) to people who do not have faith and love (the third eye).

Some people do not believe God exists at all. They are atheists. ("A" is Greek for "not" or "no", and "theos" is Greek for "God". So "a-theism" means "no God".) A theist is someone who believes God does exist.

Reason (the second eye) has ways of knowing that God exists. God's existence can be proved logically. We will explore ten of these proofs in the next chapter.

There are two reasons to know the proofs for God's existence. One is to help persuade atheists. The other is to know that faith and reason are allies, that they say the same thing. So even if you already know by faith that God exists, it's good for you to know that your reason and your faith agree.

5. What is the very best way of knowing God?

The heart gives you better knowledge of persons than the head.

The third eye, the heart, has its own ways of knowing God. Faith, hope, and love are the heart's three main ways of knowing God. They are not proofs or arguments; they are direct acknowledgements of His presence.

Faith in God means essentially trusting God. The more we trust Him, the more we know Him; the more we trust Him, the more certain we are that He is real and that He is trustable. The same principle works with human beings: the best way to know them is trust. Sometimes the *only* way to know them is trust. The more you trusted your parents as a baby, the more you knew them. And God is much more superior to us than parents are to babies. So even when we are adults, trust is the best way to know God.

Hope in God means trusting His promises. Hope is faith directed to the future.

What does loving God mean? If you love anyone totally, (a) you admire him and (b) you want to be like him, and (c) you also want to be *with* him, close to him. So loving God means first of all (a) admiring Him (in fact, totally admiring Him, because He is totally admirable, adoring Him because He is literally adorable, He is perfect). It means admiring and valuing what He is: truth and goodness. It also means (b) wanting to be like Him, wanting to be true and good. And it means (c) wanting to be close to Him, wanting to be with Him, wanting to share your life with Him, wanting to spend time with Him and talk with Him. (That's what prayer is.)

You know God better by trusting Him, hoping in Him, and loving Him than by proving His existence by reason. But you *can* prove His existence by reason. (See the next chapter.)

6. Do faith and reason ever contradict each other?

No. Never.

Remember the three ways of knowing things, the three eyes.

a. We know some things by our senses: for instance, that the sky is blue and that fire is hot.

b. We know some things by our reason: for instance, that effects need causes and that a whole cannot be smaller than any of its parts.

We also know some things, especially in science, by our reason combined with our senses: for instance, that the earth is round and that there were dinosaurs.

c. We know some things by faith (trust) in God's revelation: for instance, that Jesus will come again and that He is really present in the Eucharist.

The senses are the eyes of the body. The reason is the eye of the mind. Faith is the eye of the heart. (The heart is deeper than ordinary, surface feelings as well as deeper than the mind. The heart is at the center of the soul, as the physical heart is at the center of the body.)

All three eyes can make mistakes. But when they do not

make mistakes, when they know the truth, they do not contradict each other. Truths known by one method, or eye, can never contradict truths known by another method, or eye. For truth can never contradict truth. Only falsehood contradicts truth.

Therefore, there can never be any real contradiction between any truth known by faith and any truth known by reason or sense experience.

So if the Catholic Faith is divine revelation (as the Church and the Bible tell us it is), then nothing in it can ever contradict any truth discovered by reason. If there were any real contradiction between faith and reason, that would prove that the Faith was untrue.

You can't be a Catholic and believe that there is any contradiction between the Catholic Faith and anything reason proves to be true. For to be a Catholic is to believe the Catholic Faith, that is, to believe that it is *true*. If you believe that the Catholic religion is not true, you are not a Catholic.

You are not a Catholic just because you *like* it, or because it makes *you feel* good, or even just because it makes you *be* good and live better (though that is, of course, terribly important too). You are a Catholic because you believe Catholicism is *true*. Believing in Santa Claus made you feel good too, when you were three, and maybe your belief in Santa Claus even made you be good around Christmas time, but it's not true. You don't really believe Santa Claus exists, even though you may tell stories or sing songs about him.

If God is like Santa Claus for you, then you are an atheist, not a theist. If Jesus is like Santa Claus for you, then you are not a Christian. If the Church is like Santa Claus to you, then you are not a Catholic. The only honest reason for being a Catholic is that you believe Catholicism is *true*.

And truth never contradicts truth. So if the Catholic Faith is true, no other truth can ever contradict it, no matter how that other truth is discovered and no matter what it is. But if the bones of the dead Jesus were discovered tomorrow in a tomb outside Jerusalem, that *would* contradict the Faith. If the bones were truly Jesus' bones, that would disprove the Faith; it would prove that Jesus never really rose from the dead. But nothing like that has ever happened.

7. *But you can't prove everything in the Catholic religion, can you?*

No. You can prove some of these things, like the existence of God, but not other things, like God being a Trinity. Certain things have to be taken on faith: God revealed them, and we trust Him, for God cannot lie.

But although no one can *prove* all of the things that God has revealed (like the Trinity), no one can *dis*prove any of them either. If they were disproved, that would mean they were proved to be really false and known to be false. What you know to be false, you can't really believe. You can only pretend to.

8. *How do unbelievers try to disprove the basics of Christianity?*

Here are a few examples.

a. Atheists argue that the existence of evil in the world disproves a good and loving God. But it does not. A totally good and loving God respects our freedom to choose between good and evil. It is we who bring moral evil into the world, not God. Man, not God, invented genocide.

b. Jews and Muslims often argue that the Trinity contradicts monotheism (belief in only one God). But it does not. There is only one God, though this God is a Trinity.

c. It is sometimes argued that the doctrine of the Trinity contradicts itself, since nothing can be both one and three at the same time. But the doctrine of the Trinity does not say there is one God and three Gods, or that God is one Person and three Persons, or that God has one nature and three natures. Those would indeed be self-contradictory ideas. But the doctrine of the Trinity says that there is only one God and only one divine nature but that this one God exists in three Persons. That is a great mystery, but it is not a logical self-contradiction.

d. It is sometimes argued that it is a logical contradiction to say that Jesus is both fully divine and fully human at the same time. But that is not a contradiction. He is one Person with two natures, a divine nature and a human nature. He is not one Person and two Persons, or one nature and two natures.

Sometimes people argue that Jesus cannot have two natures, human and divine, at the same time, as Christianity says He does, because these two natures are opposites. The divine nature is immortal (God cannot die) and invisible, but it is human nature to be mortal (we can die) and visible. Since Jesus was visible and died, he must be human and not divine.

But this argument does not prove its point, for even we mere human beings have two opposite natures, visible and invisible —body and soul—at the same time. And even a human author can be both a creator and a creature at the same time when he writes an autobiography, or a novel in which he himself is one of the characters. He is both the transcendent creator of the book and one of the characters in the book he has created.

God can certainly do something similar in stepping into the story of human history.

9. But doesn't science contradict religion?

No. Never.

If science could somehow prove that God does not exist, that would contradict religion. But this has never happened.

If someone says that science has disproved religion, ask him which particular discovery of which particular science has disproved which particular teaching of which particular religion. When you get specific, you find that there is no such contradiction.

The Bible makes many historical claims that *could* possibly be disproved, but not one of them has ever been disproved. (See the chapter on the Bible for specifics.) For instance, if science or history could prove that it was not God but only Moses who invented the Ten Commandments, then Judaism as well as Christianity would be disproved. But no one has ever proved that. And if Jesus' dead bones were discovered, that would disprove the Resurrection. But no one has ever done that.

Science tells us about God's world, and religion tells us about God. True science never contradicts true religion because God's world never contradicts God. The divine Teacher wrote two textbooks: the natural world and the religion He revealed. This Teacher never contradicts Himself, so His two books never contradict each other.

10. Doesn't evolution disprove creationism?

No. There is no contradiction between the idea that God created man, as the Bible and the Catholic Faith tell us, and the idea that man's body evolved from earlier species by natural selection, as the theory of evolution tells us. For the Bible does not tell us how God made the human body. He may have made it by evolution. On the other hand, the theory of evolution does not tell us anything at all about the soul. Science does not prove that God did not create the soul out of nothing. Science cannot do that because it cannot observe the human soul with scientific instruments. Souls are invisible. Souls leave no fossils. So even if the scientific theory of evolution is true, it does not contradict the Catholic Faith. Those who say it does are misunderstanding either their science or their religion.

IV

How can you prove that God is real?

In this chapter we will change our format a bit. Instead of ten different questions, there is only one question with ten answers.

Here are ten arguments. The first nine all try to prove that a real God is the only adequate explanation for (1) the existence of the universe, (2) the order in the universe, (3) your mind, (4) your desire for happiness, (5) morality, (6) miracles, (7) the Jews, (8) saints, and (9) Jesus. All nine of these things are real only because God is real. The tenth argument (Pascal's Wager) tries to prove that it is reasonable to believe in God even if you can't prove His existence.

1. The First-Cause Argument

The universe is the sum total of everything that exists in time and space, everything made of matter. Scientists have theorized that the entire universe came into existence suddenly, at once, about fifteen billion years ago, in what they call the "Big Bang". Ever since that first moment, the universe has been expanding, growing. The *growth* of the universe is like the growth of your body; you don't need a God to explain that. Your body grows by itself. But the *existence* of the universe is like the existence of your body: your body doesn't exist by itself. It exists only because something else caused it: your parents. Like your body, the universe can make itself grow, but it can't make itself exist. (For it's not *there* before it exists, but it *is* there before it grows.) Nothing else but a Creator could have "banged out" the "Big Bang", made the whole universe. Nothing *in* the universe could have caused the universe. No *part* of the universe could have created the whole universe.

Let's go through the same argument again. This time we'll think about the principle of cause and effect in general, rather than the "Big Bang" in particular.

Nothing happens without some cause. Nothing just pops into existence for no reason at all. And the universe popped into existence. So it must have a cause.

Everything in the universe causes something else. Sunlight causes plants to grow, plant food causes animals to live, lions cause lambs to die by eating them, dogs cause puppies to be born, and so forth. The universe is like a giant chain of dominoes, each one moved by another one. If there is no finger to knock the first domino down—if there is no First Cause, if there is nothing outside the chain of dominoes, outside the universe—then no dominoes can fall. And in that case, nothing would be happening anywhere right now.

No matter how big and long and complex the chain of dominoes is, no matter how old the universe is, there has to be a First Cause to make all the other causes act. If there were no First Cause, there would be no second and third and fourth and four-billionth causes. And those second and third and fourth and four-billionth causes do exist. We see them. Therefore, there must be a First Cause, even though we do not see it.

And the absolutely First Cause of absolutely everything else is one of the things that "God" means. So we have proved the existence of God.

We have not proved very much about God yet. Is He good?

Does He love us? Is He a Trinity? We have not proved any of that. But we have disproved atheism, at least.

2. The Argument from Design

Here is a second proof. It proves not only that God exists but also that God is supremely intelligent. Basically, it argues from the design in nature to the Designer of nature.

If you see a picture, you know not only that there is a painter who caused it but also that the cause is intelligent, because the picture is ordered, intelligently designed. An animal can throw random blotches of paint on a canvas, but that is not a picture, because it has no intelligent design, no deliberate order in it. Its cause is not intelligent.

If you see a plane flying overhead, you do not think it just happened by chance. You know someone with intelligence designed the plane and is flying it.

But the universe that contains the picture and the plane has much more order and intelligent design in it than either the picture or the plane. Animal intelligence is not enough to account for pictures or planes. Only human intelligence is. But human intelligence is not enough to account for all the design in the universe. The design in the human body is so complex that every single cell in your body stores more information than all the books in all the libraries in the world. We did not invent our own bodies. We cannot even invent trees. "Poems are made by fools like me, but only God can make a tree."

If there is intelligent design, there must be an intelligent Designer.

〜

The following section is not part of the argument itself but a kind of addition to it. Science has discovered what is called the "anthropic principle". This principle means that the universe was "fine-tuned" for human life to appear. If any one of dozens of aspects of the universe had been a tiny bit different, we could never have lived. For instance, the temperature of the universe a few seconds after the Big Bang that began it was trillions of degrees hotter than the sun. If it had been a tiny bit hotter or colder, carbon molecules could never have appeared. And all life is based on carbon. If the earth had been slightly nearer the sun or slightly farther away, the plant-and-animal food cycle that supports human life could not have appeared. The same thing would have been true if the moon did not control the tides as it does or if water had a slightly higher or lower freezing point. The universe seems to be not only designed, but designed for us.

Now if "God is love", then He created and designed the universe not just for mankind in general but for each one of us, each concrete individual. For that is how love works. You can't love "humanity" because it's just an abstraction, a concept. You love real people, and they all come by ones, one at a time. So God created the universe for *you*. Think of that next time you see a sunset, and thank Him for the picture He painted to put on the walls of your mind.

When He created us, He foresaw that we would sin and that He would have to redeem us by dying for us. (Nothing takes God by surprise.) And of course, *that*—the redemption of man by the Incarnation, suffering, and death of Christ— was also done out of love: love not just for "humanity" in general but for each individual, for you, for me. If you had been the only one who sinned, He would have gone to every bit of the trouble He did in fact go through, just to save you.

It was the love of *you* that kept Him on the Cross, not the love of "humanity". It was all part of His design.

In God's world, nothing happens by chance. Not the world itself, not you, not your redemption. Nothing is blind chance, nothing is subrational; all is design. But the design is not rational in a human sense. It is an amazing, utterly unpredictable design from a divine Mind so profound and mysterious that no human mind can fully fathom it, and from a divine Heart so loving that no human heart can imagine it.

3. The Argument from the Human Brain

The most complex design in all the universe is found in the human brain. The human brain is far more sophisticated than any computer, but it resembles a computer in many ways. Now, we all know that computers don't just happen. They are designed. And the operating systems in them, the software, are also designed. So what is the cause of the design in the human brain?

There are only three possible answers. Either the brain just happened, by chance, or it was designed by intelligence; and if it was designed by intelligence, then either that intelligence was trustable, because it was wise and good, or it was not trustable, because it was dark and evil. In other words, (a) chance, (b) something like God, or (c) something like the Devil caused our brains.

But if either chance or the Devil caused our brains, we have no reason to trust them or anything they do. Would you trust a computer designed and programmed by chance, by the random throwing of marbles onto its keyboard? Would you trust one designed by a liar and a deceiver? Of course not. So unless some wise and good being, some superhuman intelligence that is totally trustable, designed the computer we always use, namely our brain, we have no reason to trust *any* of our thoughts at all, including all science and common sense and logic.

Of course, this being may have used a long, slow evolutionary process to make the human brain. Science may tell us a lot about *how* and *when* that happened but not about *who* made it happen. Science cannot see the invisible Mind of the Creator and Designer—it can see only His visible products.

4. The Argument from Desire

Everyone desires to be happy. Not just contented or satisfied (that gets boring after a while) but deeply and truly happy. In fact, we desire more than happiness—we desire *joy*. How much of it? Not just some joy, or joy mixed with some misery, but total joy. And not just for one minute or one year but forever. Ask your own heart. You can find that desire in yourself. Remember the happiest moment in your life: was it enough? Didn't it feel like the appetizer to a greater meal, or like a few sounds from a more beautiful music? And did you want that happy moment to go away? Of course not. But it did.

No one ever gets the total joy that we all long for in this life. The best life in the world is not enough. If you owned everything in the universe, you would still not be completely happy.

We all want infinite joy, and there is nothing infinite in this world. So if there is no God, if there is nothing beyond this universe, then no human being can ever find this total joy that we all most deeply want.

All the things and people we love on earth give us tastes of joy, but we want more of it. In fact, there is no limit to our desire for true joy. We have an infinite, unlimited desire for joy. We have an infinitely deep hole in our heart that needs to be filled with an infinitely deep good that can give us infinitely deep joy. Nothing but God can do that.

But what reason is there for believing there really *is* an infinitely good and loving and joy-giving God who can fill that infinite hole, can satisfy that infinite desire? Just because you have a desire for something does not mean you will get it.

That is true: just being hungry does not mean you will eat. You might starve. But being hungry *does* mean that food really exists somewhere.

Everyone has a natural and innate desire for infinite joy. That does not mean that everyone will get it. But it does mean that it exists somewhere. If there is hunger, there is food. If there is thirst, there is drink. If there is curiosity, there is knowledge. If there is loneliness, there is society. If there is sexual desire, there is sex. If ducks by nature long to swim, there must be water somewhere.

So this desire for our own complete fulfillment, our own infinite happiness and joy, is a very good reason for believing that there must be an infinitely good being who can fulfill that desire for the infinite good—in other words, God.

Saint Augustine summarized the meaning of human life beautifully in one sentence, saying to God, "You have made us for Yourself, and [that is why] our hearts are restless until they rest in You."

5. The Moral Argument

A fifth argument is the argument from morality. This argument begins with the fact that we know that some things are really right and others are really wrong. (We all know this, even when we pretend not to. There are some things we just can't not know.) We know we are under a real moral law and that we are judged by it. It is not just our subjective feelings or opinions that make things like love, justice, honesty, and courage good. They are objectively good, good in *fact*, not just good in *feeling*. They really *are* good even if they don't *feel* good. And it is not just our feelings or opinions that make things like hate, injustice, greed, dishonesty, lust, and cowardice bad. It is their real badness that makes us feel bad about them and think of them as bad, not our feeling and thinking that makes them bad.

To experience the moral law, to experience moral obligation, is to experience being *under* the moral law, not over it. We did not make the moral law that binds us all. We make civil laws, the laws of nations, and not all human beings are bound by the laws of any one nation. The laws of nations change from one nation to another and from one time to another, but the laws of true morality do not. It's never morally right, in any nation, to hate, to murder, to steal, or to commit adultery. Even if it's legal, that doesn't mean it's moral.

But how does the moral law prove God? By the principle of cause and effect. An effect has to have an adequate cause. We have seen that the moral law is not made by us but is given to us. If the moral law is given, who is its giver? Where did this real moral law come from, if not from the will of the all-good God, the perfectly moral lawgiver?

If morality came from us rather than being given to us, it would be like the rules of a game. If you made the rules, you can change them. If you agree to play nine innings of baseball and you get tired after six innings, you can change the rules and stop the game without feeling guilty. But you can't do that to morality. You can't change the rules and make good become evil and evil become good. You can't make Hitler good and Jesus evil by changing the rules. We can change the rules of games and the laws of states because we invented them in the first place. But we didn't invent human nature, so we can't change its rules.

But if the moral law does not come from us, from our minds and wills, where could it come from but from the all-good God, who created us and designed us, who designed our human nature and the moral law for human nature? Where else could morality come from? From something *less* than us? From chance? From animal instincts? From the need to survive physically? No, for how could something less than us have such authority over us?

Let's go through the two steps of this argument once more: (a) morality is real, (b) therefore, God is real.

a. Everyone admits that true morality has authority. Everyone admits that you should never disobey your moral conscience. Even people who don't believe we all stand under the same objectively real moral law, even people who believe that morality is merely subjective and can vary completely from one person to another—even these people believe in this one moral absolute, at least: always obey your conscience. It's always morally wrong to deliberately disobey your conscience.

b. But why? What gives moral conscience such absolute authority? If conscience is the voice of God speaking to each human heart, that explains why conscience has such authority. But nothing else explains it. If conscience is only the voice of society, or of your parents, why must you always obey it? Society is not always right. Parents are not always right. If conscience is only a feeling, or an instinct, why must you always obey this feeling or instinct rather than other ones? None of our other feelings or instincts has that absolute authority. Nothing less than God can explain the absolute moral authority of conscience. Morality is real because God is real.

6. The Argument from Miracles

Our sixth argument is the argument from miracles: if miracles happen, they must have a cause. Everything that happens has an adequate cause. But a miracle is an event that nothing in nature can cause. For instance, no force in nature can bring back the dead. The only adequate cause of a miracle is a supernatural being.

But miracles do happen. There is plenty of good evidence for them. For instance, there is much evidence for Jesus' Resurrection. (See chapter VI.) Therefore, there must be a miracle worker, and only God is literally a miracle worker.

7. The Argument from the Jews

The Jews are history's biggest public miracle. By every known law of human history, they should have perished many times. Long lines of tyrants from ancient Egypt's pharaoh to modern Germany's Hitler have tried to wipe them out. Yet they have survived and thrived. They have contributed far more to

Western civilization than any other people, even though they are far less in number than hundreds of other peoples. They stand out as no other people has ever stood out in all human history.

This is a fact. And there are only two possible explanations: either the Jews are responsible for their success or God is. The Jews' claim (and the Bible's) is that it is God's doing, that God chose them, that they are His "chosen people". This is really the humblest possible explanation of the fact, for the only other explanation is that they did it all by themselves.

Half the world today believes in the God of the Jews: over two billion Christians and over a billion Muslims. No one else knows God as one, infinitely powerful, infinitely wise, infinitely good Creator, Revealer, and Person (I AM).

Most of the world also believes in the Ten Commandments, which are the moral basis for Western civilization. No moral law has ever been as perfect, as perfectly preserved, and as powerful and persuasive as these commandments that God gave to the Jews through Moses.

How did the Jews convince over three billion people to believe in their God and His laws? Was that their doing, or was that God's doing?

8. The Argument from the Saints

If there is no God, then the saints are the biggest fools in history, because next to Jesus himself, they are the closest to Him and the most intimate with Him. If there is no God, then the better and more saintly you are, the more wrong you are, the more stupid you are about life and its meaning.

If there is no God, then everyone's two deepest desires contradict each other: the desire to be good and the desire to be wise, the desire for moral goodness and the desire for truth and knowledge. For if there is no God, then the more saintly you get, the more you believe in this nonexistent God and trust Him and love Him. In other words, the more *good* you get, the more stupid you get, the more you live a lie, a falsehood, an illusion, like a grownup still believing in a four-year-old's invisible playmate.

Albert Camus, the great French novelist, was an atheist who deeply worried about this puzzle. In his novel *The Plague*, he has his hero, Dr. Rieux, risk his life to save thousands of people from a deadly plague, because Dr. Rieux believes that the meaning of life is to be a saint. He also believes that you can't be a saint without God. But Dr. Rieux is an atheist and believes that there is no real God. One of those three beliefs must be false. No one can live with that puzzle for long. Either he will have to come to believe in God as the saint-maker, or he will have to stop believing in sanctity. You *can* be both a moral person and an atheist at the same time, but it will eventually tear you apart inside if you think about it deeply, as Camus did.

But the best form of the argument from the saints is not just thinking about the puzzle of how you can be a saint without God, but *meeting* some truly saintly persons. Go meet Mother Teresa's Missionaries of Charity or some Carmelite contemplative monks or nuns, and you will *see* it. The wisdom and the happiness just shines from their eyes.

9. The Argument from Jesus

If there is no God, then Jesus Christ, the most admired man in history, is really the biggest fool in history. For no one made

God more important in his life than He did. No one's teaching depended more on God's reality than His teaching did. No one was as dependent on God as He was.

Everyone admires His Teaching. But He said that His teaching was not his own but was from His Father, God. Everyone admires His moral goodness, His goodwill. But He said that He came into the world not to do His own will but the will of His Father. If God the Father does not exist, Jesus is insane—as insane as a forty-year-old man who still believes in the Tooth Fairy, prays to the Tooth Fairy, never does anything unless the Tooth Fairy tells him to, teaches only what the Tooth Fairy teaches, and tries to get everyone in the world to believe in the Tooth Fairy and love the Tooth Fairy and trust the Tooth Fairy to give them salvation and eternal life and complete happiness.

And you can make the argument from Jesus much stronger than words, in the same way as you can make the argument from the saints much stronger than words: by meeting Him. Read the Gospels, as if you had never read them before. Imagine you are one of the first-century Jews who met Jesus for the first time. If you let yourself *meet* Him, you will see. You will not see insanity.

10. Pascal's Wager

Our last argument does not prove that God exists, but it proves that believing in God is much more reasonable than not believing in God. The argument is called "Pascal's Wager", after Pascal, a seventeenth-century French philosopher, scientist, and mathematician. He invented the world's first working computer among many other things, such as the vacuum cleaner and public transportation. Try reading his *Pensées* sometime. They are one thousand short but striking little notes about the meaning of life written for ordinary people, not specialists.

Atheists can't be *certain* there is no God. Most of them are really agnostics rather than atheists. "A-gnosis" in Greek means "no-knowledge". An agnostic is one who does not know whether or not there is a God, or one who claims that no one can know whether there is a God.

If you do not know whether God exists or not, what is the reasonable thing to do?

If there is no proof, you have to take a chance. You wager. You bet for or against God.

But betting that there is a God is the only bet that can ever pay off. If God exists and you bet on Him, look what you can win: God! But if He exists and you bet against Him, you've lost Him. He offered you eternal life for free, and you turned it down.

But what if He doesn't exist? Then there's nothing to win and nothing to lose, so it makes no difference in the end.

So, according to Pascal, the only possible way to win is to bet for Him, and the only possible way to lose is to bet against Him. Believing in God is the best bet in the world.

If you don't know whether God exists or not, what should you do? If you don't *know* the truth, you should *seek* the truth. Wonder. Look. Inquire. Seek. Even if you don't believe in Jesus, you can believe in Jesus' promise, "Seek and you shall find." You can't even be a scientist without believing that, for science means seeking the truth about nature because you hope to find it. So let's use the same principle about seeking the truth about whether there is a God. Let's really look! Let's look for evidence, for data.

Where shall we look? If you wonder whether atoms exist, perform the appropriate experiment: look at molecules under electron microscopes in laboratories. If you wonder whether the Loch Ness Monster exists, perform the appropriate experiment: go to Loch Ness and explore it with submarines and cameras. If you wonder whether monkeys can be taught to talk, perform the appropriate experiment: get some monkeys and try to teach them. If you wonder whether selfishness exists, perform the appropriate experiment: look into your own heart and life. And if you wonder whether God exists, perform the appropriate experiment: pray.

You can pray even if you are an agnostic or a sceptic. You can pray "the prayer of the sceptic": "God, I don't know whether You exist or not. I may be praying to nothing. But I may be praying to a real You. So if You are real, please let me find You. Because even though I don't know whether You exist or not, I do know that I ought to be honest and that I ought to believe whatever is the truth."

Jesus said, "Seek and you shall find." If we truly believe that, then we should dare to say to the sceptic that if he is truly honest and prays that prayer, it is certain that he will eventually find the truth. Challenge him: "What are you afraid of?"

V

Why believe the Bible?

1. Isn't the whole Christian religion based on some old stories in old books that are myths that modern science has debunked? How do we know what Jesus really said? How do we know He performed miracles? How do we know He rose from the dead? How do we know He founded a Church? How do we know Jesus even existed? Only because we assume that the Bible is true. But the existence of Jesus is only an idea, an opinion, a belief. It may be true or it may be false, but it's only an opinion, not a fact. And it's also an old idea or opinion, a prescientific idea.

There are four mistakes in this argument.

a. The first mistake is the most important one. Our faith is not based on human ideas or opinions. It is based on the reality of God. God is not an idea any more than you are. The reality of God is a fact, just as much as the reality of you is a fact. God is not real because we believe in Him; we believe in Him because He is real. You are not real because your friend believes in you; your friend believes in you because you are real.

(Of course, the way your friend knows you are real is not the same as the way you know God is real. Your friend can see you, but you can't see God, because you are confined to a physical body, and God is not.)

b. The second mistake is the assumption that old ideas cannot be just as reliable as new ideas. In fact, old ideas can be even more reliable, for they have stood the test of time.

You can't find out whether an idea is true or false just by finding out whether it's old or new. Some old ideas are true, and some are false. Some new ideas are true, and some are false. You don't tell the truth by a calendar or a clock.

In fact, if you think all old ideas are false just because they're old, that makes you a kind of snob. A snob is someone who feels superior to another class of people and is prejudiced against them. If it's stupid to be prejudiced against some class of people in the present, then it's also stupid to be prejudiced against all people in the past. If it's stupid to be a snob, it's also stupid to be a historical snob.

c. The third mistake is the assumption that the historical stories in the Bible are myths, like fairy tales. They are not. They are historical accounts handed down from eyewitnesses. People *saw* the Red Sea part; people *saw* Jesus perform miracles.

People who do not believe miracles can ever happen often interpret the Bible's miracle stories as myths instead of facts. But that's confusing *interpretation* with *belief*. What you believe is dependent on *you*; your beliefs are *your* ideas. But your *interpretation* of someone else's words should be dependent on that *other* person's ideas. Interpretation means trying to find out what the other person meant, not what you would have meant. The authors of the Bible are trying to communicate their ideas to you. Listen!

The miracle stories in the Bible cannot be interpreted as myths because they claim to be facts. The Bible explicitly says they are not myths: "For we did not follow cleverly devised myths when we made known to you the power and coming of our Lord Jesus Christ, but we were eyewitnesses of his majesty" (2 Pet 1:16). The Gospels are either deliberate lies or facts. These events either happened, or they didn't. If they happened, they are facts. If they didn't, then the Bible's claims that they did is a lie.

This is especially true of Jesus' Resurrection. First Corinthians 15:14, 17 says: "If Christ has not been raised, then our preaching is in vain and your faith is in vain. . . . If Christ has not been raised, your faith is futile and you are still in your sins."

d. The fourth mistake is the assumption that our faith *begins* with the Bible. You don't have to prove the Bible is true first, and then prove from the Bible that the Church is true, and then prove from the Church that Jesus is true, and then prove from Jesus that God is true. It's the other way around. You start with God. You believe in Jesus because He is God. You believe in the Church because she is Jesus' Church. You believe in the Bible because it is the Church's book.

If you don't believe in God first, you won't believe that Jesus is God. If you don't believe that Jesus is God, you won't believe the Church He established is God's Church. If you don't believe in the Church, you won't believe in her book, the New Testament, because the Church's apostles wrote it and the Church later "canonized" it—that is, defined it, said which books were part of it, part of the "canon" or list of books that are divine revelation.

The Gospel was preached before it was written down. The first generation of Christians had no New Testament, no *written* Gospel. They believed the *spoken* Gospel, the testimony of Jesus' apostles and their successors—in other words, the Church. The primary object of our faith is not the Bible but the facts; not the four Gospels but the Gospel. "Gospel" means "good news". "News" means facts. The Bible is only the newspaper.

Let's go through this again, point by point.

a. God is real.

b. God revealed Himself in a special way to the Jewish people, through miracles and through prophets. The Old Testament records this history.

c. Among these Jews, Jesus appeared and claimed to be God.

d. Jesus chose twelve apostles. They saw and heard the events later recorded in the Gospels.

e. Jesus authorized the apostles to teach in His name (Lk 10:16), and in His name they appointed successors. These successors are the bishops of the one Catholic (universal) Church, the Church that Jesus founded.

f. The apostles preached the "good news" about Christ, and many believed. Later, some of these apostles and disciples wrote the New Testament, so that after they died, all the people in the world, till the end of time, could know exactly what happened when the most important event in history occurred: God became man in Jesus.

So our faith does not *begin* with the Bible. But the Bible records the realities, the real events, that are the basis of our faith.

2. *But wasn't the Bible written in an old, prescientific style, the style of myth?*

No, most of it was not. The Bible is different from all other religious literature because it records historical facts, real events that were actually seen by eyewitnesses. It is simply a literary fact that most of the Bible, especially the Gospels, has a very different literary style than the pagan myths. You can see that for yourself by comparing the two.

Actually, the word "myth" can be used in at least three different ways, and we should distinguish these three meanings when we speak about the Bible.

a. When we say of something that it's a "myth", we often mean simply that it's not true, that it's a lie that some people are "suckered into" and deceived by—for instance, the myth that the ancient Roman emperors were gods, or that Communism was a political system that helped the poor, or that George Washington once threw a silver dollar across the Potomac River.

b. At other times, we mean by a "myth" something that's not *literally* true but *is symbolically* true. It's not meant to be a lie or a deception. For instance, Aesop's fables, stories about talking animals, are myths. Animals don't really talk, and Aesop doesn't try to deceive us into thinking that they do, but his stories use the myth of talking animals to teach true moral principles. So do many other children's stories about talking animals.

c. Sometimes, even real historical events can be told in mythic, symbolic, nonliteral language. When we say "George Washington was the father of his country", we don't mean it literally, physically, biologically. We use symbolic language. We often do this even when we narrate real historical events.

Now let's apply these three meanings of myth to the Bible.

a. The Bible does not contain any myths in the first sense. It rejects them. For instance, the pagan gods and the religions that worshipped them are rejected by the Bible as false, as deceptions, as lies.

b. The Bible does contain some mythical stories that aren't meant to be taken literally, such as the parables told by Jesus. They are fiction with a moral message. Perhaps Noah's ark, the story of Job, and the story of Jonah and the whale are meant to be moral parables rather than narrations of historical events. (These three are borderline cases; some good Bible scholars believe they are historical narratives, while others believe they are meant as moral fables.)

c. The Bible often uses myth in the third sense, narrating real historical events in symbolic language. For instance, in the creation story in Genesis, the Bible says that God created the world in six "days". These are not meant to be interpreted as literal, twenty-four-hour days because in this same Genesis creation story, it says that the sun and moon are not made until the fourth "day", and the author knew that the sun and moon measure our literal days and months. He was writing in the Hebrew language, and in Hebrew, the word for "day" (*yom*) often means simply the appointed time for something. For instance, the "day of the Lord", *Yom Adonai*, means the time when God's promised Messiah comes to establish His Kingdom. That "day" has lasted for two thousand years so far, not just twenty-four hours.

Yet the creation of the world was a real, historical event. It is not like stories of talking animals. It really happened.

The same is true about the end of the world. It will really happen. But the book of Revelation tells the story of the end of the world in a highly symbolic way. For instance, the author did not mean for us to interpret the four horsemen in the sky as four cowboys whose horses acted like airplanes!

3. But the Bible was written by primitive people who didn't know modern science. How can we trust it?

If the Bible claimed to be a science textbook, it would indeed be a primitive one. But that is not its purpose.

The Bible does, however, speak about real people, places, and events. It makes many claims about historical events that can be checked out by science—more than any other religious book does. Other religious books, like the scriptures of Hinduism, Buddhism, or Islam, mention very few historical events. They teach timeless theological truths (or, perhaps, falsehoods) and moral principles and speak of private religious and mystical experiences, but science can't prove or disprove any of those, because science can prove or disprove only historical facts. The Bible mentions thousands of historical facts, and science has never refuted a single one.

4. But the Bible is only a book, after all, not a historical fact.

Books are historical facts too, just as much as the people who write them.

Books are humanity's most reliable way of passing information down through time and across space.

Both the Bible and Jesus are called the "Word of God". The Bible is the Word of God on paper; Jesus is the Word of God in flesh.

A person is more than a book, and Jesus is more than the Bible. A book points to a person, and the Bible points to Jesus.

5. *But the Bible writers were writing to people who were ignorant of the facts of history. They were gullible: they could believe anything.*

This is an example of "historical snobbery". (See page 62.) It is simply not true. Most cultures in the past took their history much *more* seriously than we do. They preserved and treasured and remembered their history with great care. Many people today are much more gullible and ignorant of history than the people in Bible times were. For instance, many people who read Dan Brown's novel *The Da Vinci Code* believe that this piece of fiction could have been historical fact. They believe the ridiculous ideas that this novel presents as real history: for instance, that none of Jesus' followers for the first three hundred years believed that Jesus was divine until the emperor Constantine invented the idea in A.D. 313 for his own selfish purposes to get political power. That's as ridiculous as saying that Communism wasn't invented until 1965, by Fidel Castro. All the data refute it. The belief that Jesus is divine is found in almost every single one of the thousands of books that were written by Christians between the death of Christ (ca. A.D. 30) and the time of Constantine (A.D. 313), starting with the twenty-seven books of the New Testament. Only historically ignorant and gullible people could believe such myths as *The Da Vinci Code*.

6. *The Bible is only words. Does God speak in* words? *Aren't feelings more important?*

Words are the way we communicate with each other. So God used our language to communicate with us. If He had used anything else, like mystical experiences, it would have been private, not public; only a few people would "get it".

Of course feelings are important, but so are words. For feelings are expressed and communicated by words. (Feelings are also *created* by words, for instance—"I love you" or "I hate you.")

Words communicate facts as well as feelings. And if feelings aren't in line with facts, they can be destructive. A Chinese parable puts it this way: Fact, Faith, and Feeling are three people walking along a wall. As long as Faith keeps his eyes on Fact, all three keep walking. But when Faith takes his eyes off Fact and turns around to worry about how Feeling is doing, both Faith and Feeling fall off the wall, while Fact marches on. Our faith is not based on feelings but on facts.

Or, to change the image, feelings are like flowers, faith is like stems, and facts are like roots. The flowers are beautiful, but they are based on the stems, and the stems are based on the roots. This is true about our relationships to each other as well as our relationship with God. For instance, you feel affection toward your parents because you have faith that they love you, and you feel fear toward a screaming man running at you with a knife because you believe he wants to kill you. Those two beliefs, in turn, are based on objective facts. First fact, then faith, then feeling.

7. *How could God write the Bible? He's a spirit. Men wrote the Bible. You can see their human personalities in their writing.*

Of course you can, and of course they did. But God inspired them.

The Bible, like Jesus, has two natures, divine and human. It is the Word of God in the words of men. It is like white light shining through a stained glass window with many colors.

What was the role of God and what was the role of the human authors in writing the Bible? There are three possible answers to that question, three theories about the role of God and the role of the human authors in writing the Bible.

"Fundamentalist" theologians usually believe that God dictated the Bible word for word, without the human author having any input.

"Liberal" or "Modernist" theologians believe that the Bible is only man's best words about God, not God's words about man.

The third answer is the one the Catholic Church teaches: that God providentially used human authors, and their human personalities, with all their human limitations, but "inspired" them and providentially kept them from making errors about religion. (Since the Bible does not claim to teach grammar or science or math, God did not correct human errors in those areas.)

There are two basic heresies (falsehoods, errors, mistakes) about Jesus: that He was only human and not divine, and that He was only divine and not human. There are also the same two mistakes about the Bible: that it is only human and not divinely inspired, and that it is only divine and not human.

8. *Who knows how to interpret the Bible, anyway? Everybody interprets it in his own way. You get out of it whatever you put into it.*

Two answers:

    a. That's why we need the Church. The Church knows how

to interpret the Bible. The Church is like a living teacher, and the Bible is her textbook.

b. We should not interpret the Bible, *or any other book*, in our own way but in the author's way. We should first listen, as in conversation. A book is a conversation between the writer and the reader. We all know people who just keep talking and don't listen. Don't be like them when you read a book. Let it do the talking first, then talk back. Don't interpret a book—any book, including the Bible—according to your own ideas. Interpret it according to the author's ideas. Then you'll get out of it *more* than you put into it: you'll get the author's mind out of it, not just your own.

9. *Haven't there been mistakes in translation? How do we know the Bible we have today is the same book the authors originally wrote?*

The text of the Bible was transmitted (handed down, copied) very, very carefully. Before printing was invented, it was copied by hand. Jewish copiers were so careful that they copied the exact size and shape of each letter of each Hebrew word, as well as the right letter!

All later translations into all other languages can be checked by going back to the oldest copies that we have in the two original languages: Hebrew for the Old Testament, and Greek for the New Testament. And we have earlier copies, and many more of them, for the Bible than for any other premodern book in the world. So we can check out the text very scientifically. And when we do, we find that there are very few discrepancies, or differences, or disagreements, between the many different copies, and that none of the differences is terribly important.

10. *What* is *the proper use of the Bible? Who are the ones who use it best? Hasn't the Bible been terribly misused and abused throughout history?*

Yes. And the way to avoid that is to use it rightly, not to refuse to use it at all. There is a Latin maxim, *abusus non tollit usum*: "abuse does not take away use." The abuse of any good thing does not take away the proper use of that thing. And those who use it best are the saints.

～

Some suggested Bible readings:

> Genesis, especially chapters 1 and 3
> Exodus 1–20
> Psalms, especially 1, 8, 19, 23, 24, 42, 51, 90, 91, 103,
>   137, 139, 150
> The four Gospels
> Romans 8
> 1 Corinthians 13 and 15

VI

Why is Jesus different?

1. The different religions of the world were founded by different people: Moses, Jesus, Muhammad, Buddha, Confucius, Lao Tzu. How is Jesus different from the others? Also, the teachings of all the religions of the world agree about many things. Is there anything totally and radically different in the teachings of Christianity? Is there anything that all Christians believe but no one else believes?

The answers to these questions are found in the earliest creed in the history of Christianity.

Creeds are summaries of belief. There have been many creeds in the history of Christianity. The long one we recite at Mass every Sunday is the Nicene Creed, which was formulated in the fourth century. The shorter one we say at the beginning of the Rosary is the Apostles' Creed, which was formulated in the early second century and stems from the teaching of the twelve apostles. But there is one even earlier and shorter creed, which is mentioned twice in the New Testament itself. (See 1 Cor 12:3 and Phil 2:11.) It consists of only three words:

"Jesus is Lord."

The Greek word translated "Lord", *kyrios*, means "God", not any merely human lord, like a king or a master of servants. "Jesus is Lord" means "Jesus is God." This is the essential belief of Christianity.

73

2. *What makes this belief different from those of other religions?*

The same thing that makes the center point of a circle different from all other points on the circle. This is the center of Christianity. Christianity is *Christ*-ianity.

"Christ" means the "Messiah", or the "anointed one"—the "promised one", the one promised by the Jewish prophets. "Christ" is His *title*. His given *name* is Jesus. "Jesus" means "Savior", or "God saves". God's angel told Joseph, "You shall call his name Jesus, for he will save his people from their sins" (Mt 1:21).

The center of Christianity is Jesus because Jesus is not just a great human being; Jesus is God. The center of Islam is *not* Muhammad, because Muhammad, like Moses, claimed only to be a prophet, not God. The center of Buddhism is not Buddha, because Buddha, like the Hindu gurus, claimed only to be an "enlightened" man, not God. ("Buddha" means the "man who woke up".) The center of Confucianism is not Confucius, because Confucius, like other Chinese philosophers, claimed only to be a teacher and a moral reformer, not God. But Jesus is the center of Christianity because Jesus claimed to be God, and Christians believe that claim.

Jesus is the center because Jesus is God, and God is the center—the center of reality. Jesus is the center *because God is real*.

The divinity of Christ is *the* distinctive Christian belief: it is the one thing all Christians believe and no one else does. If a Christian ceases to believe this, he ceases to be a Christian. If a non-Christian comes to believe this, he becomes a Christian.

Jesus is God, literally. He is not just *like* God, or close to God, or Godly but is God Himself, in person, in human flesh.

3. *It seems ridiculous to believe that literally. How can a man be God? How can God be a man?*
   God is the Creator of the universe; man is only a creature within the universe.
   God is immortal; man is mortal. (God cannot die; man can die.)
   God has no beginning; man has a beginning. (God is not born; God has no mother. Man is born; every man has a mother.)
   God is a pure spirit; man has a physical body. (God is invisible; man is visible.)
   So it seems like a logical contradiction for Jesus to be both God and man at the same time.

It is not a logical *contradiction* but a *paradox*. A paradox is an *apparent* contradiction that is not *really* a contradiction.

Here is a similar (but not identical) paradox in our own experience: you yourself are both spirit and matter, both soul and body, both visible and invisible. Can I see you? Yes *and* no. I can see your body; I cannot see your soul. Yet you are only one person, not two. You, the one and only you, the individual you, the one person you call "yourself", are both visible and invisible at the same time. Human nature already includes within itself these two opposite attributes. So it is not simply impossible and unthinkable for one person (Jesus) to have two natures that are opposite, namely a human nature and a divine nature, for human nature already includes opposites.

This can happen—God can become a man without ceasing to be God—because God can do anything! He is omnipotent, or all-powerful. There is no limit to His power.

(The only things God cannot do are things that are literally meaningless. For instance, He cannot both exist and not exist, or both give us free will and not give us free will at the same time, or both perform a miracle and not perform a miracle at the same time, or make a rock bigger than He can lift, bigger than infinite power can lift. There can be no such rock.)

So God can become man without ceasing to be God. It is not meaningless and impossible, like making a rock bigger than He can lift. There is even a human analogy for this. (An analogy is one thing that is a bit like a second thing but not exactly the same.) The analogy is this: a human storyteller can put himself into his own story as one of his characters. He can write a true autobiography. Or a human moviemaker can put himself into one of his own movies as one of the actors. (Alfred Hitchcock did exactly that in his old thriller movies. You can see him briefly walking across the street as a pedestrian in some of his movies. See if you can spot him. He looks like a well-dressed penguin.)

So there is no reason why God can't put Himself into the universe He created. If a man can do it, God can certainly do it. The God who invented all of human history, as a moviemaker invents a movie, can put Himself into His story as one of His own "characters" just as much as Alfred Hitchcock can. The difference, of course, is that when God makes the universe, it's not just a fictional story, like a movie, but real, and all the characters are real too: as real as you are.

God can do this *because God is real*. He can make a real universe because He is real, and He can become a real man (Jesus) because He is real. If He created the whole universe out of nothing, He can certainly step into His own created universe if He wants to.

If a Martian came to earth, he would have to leave Mars. But for God to come to earth, He does not need to leave Heaven, because Heaven isn't some place in the universe, as Mars is. Heaven is more like the Mind of the Creator of the universe.

Remember the analogy of the writer of the autobiography, or the moviemaker. The creator can step into his created work without leaving any other place. Alfred Hitchcock doesn't need to leave his movie studio to come into his movie. For it's the movie studio that *makes* the movie. So that character in the movie, that one person, Alfred Hitchcock, is at the same time both the maker of the movie, outside it, *and* one of the characters in it, inside it. Similarly, Jesus is at the same time God, the maker of the universe, the divine Creator, *and* a man, one of the creatures in it, when He "incarnates" or puts Himself into it.

This is the Christian doctrine (teaching) that is called the "Incarnation". "Incarnation" means literally the "enfleshing" of God, God (the second Person of the Trinity; the divine, eternal Father's divine, eternal Son) becoming a literal flesh-and-blood man named Jesus without ceasing to be God. The Incarnation happened nine months before Jesus' birth, when Mary gave God her free consent to do this astonishing thing, after God's angel announced it to her, at the Annunciation. Jesus was a tiny human being in Mary's womb for nine months. He grew as all human beings grow, as a human embryo, fetus, infant, child, teenager, and finally adult.

4. *But even if it is* possible *for God to do this, why do Christians believe He actually did it? Is there any proof that it happened? Is there any reason for believing it? Is there any evidence for it? How do you know it's true? It's just a subjective belief in your mind; there are no objective data, or facts, or evidence, are there?*

Yes! There is very good reason for believing it. There is evidence. There are data.

Let's begin with what we have already learned:

a. God is real. We established that in chapter IV.

b. This God is not just one of the many gods of the pagan myths, like Zeus, who are only finite *parts* of the cosmos or universe. For instance, in Greek mythology, Zeus lives on Mount Olympus, Poseidon lives in the sea, and Apollo takes care of the sun. But God is the infinite, transcendent *Creator* of the universe.

Nor is God the God of pantheism, the God who is simply everything in general and nothing in particular, the God who is the whole cosmos, or the spirit of the whole cosmos, or the impersonal Energy or "cosmic consciousness" in everything, like the "Force" in *Star Wars*. God is not the universe, and He is not "in" the universe as space is in the universe. He is the Creator of the universe. He is not the whole, He is more: He is the transcendent Creator of the whole.

c. God revealed Himself to one people that He chose (the Jews) to be His collective prophet to the world, so that the whole world might come to know the true God. Jews, Christians, and Muslims accept that revelation.

d. Now, among the Jews, a man turns up who claims to be God. He was a Jew. When He talked about God, He meant by "God" the God of the Jews, not one of the many gods of the Greeks, like Zeus, or the pantheistic "everything" God of the Hindus, whose name was Brahman. He meant what all the Jews meant by "God". He meant the one, personal, infinite, transcendent, perfect, righteous Creator. Jesus was not a Greek or a Hindu but a Jew. That is simply a historical fact.

But unlike all the other Jews, He called God His Father. He called Himself the "only Son of God" as well as the "Son of man". What did He mean by this?

It's not hard to understand what He meant. The son of a man is a man, and the son of God is God. Human fathers give human nature to their children; God the Father gives divine nature to His Son. So when Jesus called Himself the "Son of God", He was calling Himself God. When "doubting Thomas" finally confessed Him as "my Lord and my God", Jesus accepted this title (Jn 20:28–29).

Jesus called God His Father. But there are three important differences between divine fatherhood and human fatherhood. First, when human parents produce human children, they do this in time, in a progression of before-and-after: first comes the parents, then the child. Second, human fathers need human mothers to make children. They can't do it alone. Third, human parents need bodies. They can't just think children into existence. But God the Father begets God the Son without time, without a wife, and without a body. He does it eternally, without beginning or end, and even without any before-and-after change. God the Son is *eternally* begotten from God the Father.

Jesus has a divine Father but not a divine mother. And He has a human mother (Mary) but not a human father. Joseph was only His foster-father. Mary was a virgin when she conceived Jesus. Jesus took His divine nature from His divine Father, who was His only Father, and He took His human nature from His human mother Mary, who was His only mother. He has no divine mother and no human father.

Jesus claimed to be divine in many different ways. For instance, when the Jews demanded that He tell them just who He claimed to be, He said, "Truly, truly, I say to you, before Abraham was, I AM" (Jn 8:58). "I AM" was the name God called Himself when He revealed Himself to Moses in the burning bush (Ex 3:14). It was a name so sacred that no Jew would even pronounce it. It was blasphemy to speak that word. Only God could speak it, for to say "I AM" is to claim to *be* "I AM". All other names (like "Zeus" or "Joe") can be spoken *to*. If I say "Zeus" or "Joe", I do not claim to *be* Zeus or Joe. But if I say "I", I mean myself, not someone else. And Jesus spoke this forbidden word, deliberately. The Jews clearly understood that this was a claim to be God, for as soon as Jesus said this, they picked up stones and tried to stone Him to death (Jn 8:59), for that was the penalty for blasphemy under Mosaic law, and it is the height of blasphemy for a mere man to claim to be God.

Another way Jesus claimed to be God was in His claim to forgive sins—all sins, any sins, against anybody. The Jews understood that this was a claim to be God, for when they heard this, they said, "Who can forgive sins but God alone?" I have a right to forgive you for your sins against me—for instance, if you steal money from me, I have a right to forgive you for it if I want to—but I have no right to forgive you for stealing Harry's money. Only Harry has that right. So why could Jesus forgive you for stealing Harry's money? Because when you sin against Harry, you also sin against God, because God is the giver of the moral law "Thou shalt not steal", and God is the one who is offended in all sins against all people because God alone is the Father and Creator of all people. We are all God's children, and to sin against His children is to sin against Him. So Jesus said what God alone had a right to say: "*I* forgive you for *all* your sins, against everybody."

5. *Okay, so Jesus* claimed *to be God. But just claiming it doesn't prove it. It's still not a* fact *that Jesus is God; the only fact is that he* claimed *to be God. But his* really being *God isn't a fact; it's only a faith.*

It's true that just claiming something to be so doesn't prove it is so. And it's true that believing His claim is faith. But this faith is also totally reasonable.

For how else can we explain the fact that Jesus claimed to be God? That claim, in the Gospels, is our data. Let's be scientific; let's look at our data and let's insist on explaining our data.

There are only two possible explanations. Either

a. Jesus spoke the truth, or
b. Jesus did not speak the truth.

In other words, either

a. Jesus was, and is, God, as He claimed to be, or else
b. Jesus was not God, even though He claimed to be.

Those are the only two possibilities. So if we eliminate (b), we are left with (a). If we prove (b) is false, then we prove that (a) is true.

So let's look at (b). This is what all non-Christians believe: that Jesus is not God, only a man.

They always say He was a good man, a great man. But what kind of a man is He if He is not God but claimed to be God? He is a man who did not tell the truth about Himself. That is not a good man, certainly not a great man.

There are only two reasons why anyone does not speak the truth: either he knows he is not speaking the truth, or he doesn't know he is not speaking the truth. If a man knows he is not speaking the truth, he is deceiving us. If he doesn't know it, he is deceived himself. So he is either a deceiver or deceived. He is either deliberately lying or sincerely mistaken.

But what kind of a lie would this be, and what kind of a mistake would this be? The worst lie in the world, and the worst mistake in the world. If it's a lie, and he wants us to believe it, if he wants us to worship him as God and trust him with our lives, our selves, our souls, and our eternal salvation, even though he knows that is a lie, what kind of a liar is that? That is not just a fibber but a wicked, conniving, evil, blaspheming deceiver, like the Devil.

And if it's not a deliberate lie but a sincere mistake, then it's not just a mistake but a literally *insane* mistake, in fact the most insane mistake anyone can ever make about himself. If your brother actually believed he was God, the infinitely wise, infinitely powerful, infinitely good Creator of the universe, you would certainly say he was insane. You would send him to a psychiatrist or put him into a mental hospital. Is that what Jesus needs? Admission into an insane asylum?

So if Jesus isn't the Lord, then He's either the world's biggest liar or the world's biggest lunatic.

Why would anyone trust either the world's biggest liar or the world's biggest lunatic? Why would parents send their kids to religion class to learn about him? Why would anyone admire him? Why would everyone say his teachings were wise and good and the best way to live? Why believe the teachings of the world's biggest liar or the world's biggest lunatic?

There are only three possibilities: Jesus was (a) the Lord (as He claimed to be), (b) a liar, or (c) a lunatic. If He is not a liar or a lunatic, He must be the Lord. The one and only thing He cannot possibly be is the thing all non-Christians say He is: a good man but not God. If He is not God, He is not a good man but a bad man, in fact a very bad man indeed. He is either morally bad (a very big liar) or mentally bad (a very big lunatic).

Can anyone read the Gospels and see Jesus as a liar or a lunatic? Look at His wisdom, His goodness, His love, His power to attract people. Even non-Christians say He was good and wise—in fact, many say He was the best and wisest man who ever lived. He was beautiful! Liars are not beautiful, and lunatics are not beautiful.

Look at His personality. Read the Gospels, not what other people say about them. Look at the data. Get to know Him. He's like Aslan in *The Lion, the Witch and the Wardrobe*: He's "not *tame*, but He's *good*." He's not goody-goody; He's good. He's not just gentle but also strong. He's not like a soft, squooshy, comfortable teddy bear but more like a lion. He surprises people. He offends people, especially wicked and dishonest people. Just like reality does. Your dreams never do that. But reality does. Jesus does that because He's real, for God is real.

6. *Maybe the so-called data are all fiction. Maybe Jesus didn't lie, but the Gospels lie. Maybe Jesus never even claimed to be God, as the Gospels say He did. Maybe the story in the Gospels is just a man-made myth, a piece of fantasy. Maybe the miracle stories and the story of the Resurrection are science fiction.*

If that is so, then the Gospel is by far the most incredible, amazing piece of fantasy or science fiction ever invented. If the Jesus of the Gospels is only fiction, then why does He seem more real than any real people that we know?

If Jesus were a myth, then who were the mythmakers? Matthew, Mark, Luke, and John? *They* invented the world's greatest fantasy novel almost two thousand years before Tolkien? And not just one of them but four of them? (There are four Gospels, remember.)

That's harder to believe than Christianity. It takes a lot more faith to believe *that* than it takes to believe that Jesus is God. Even today, after 2,000 years of Christianity, it is impossible to write convincing fiction about the true Jesus. Who could have invented Him in the first place?

7. *Maybe Jesus never even existed. Who knows what really happened way back then? Anything is possible.*

No, it isn't. Do you think it's possible that George Washington never existed? Or that Julius Caesar was really not a Roman emperor at all? Of course not. Why not? Because we have historical data: we have an unbroken, uniform tradition, and we have hundreds of documents.

And we have an even more massive unbroken, uniform tradition, and *thousands* of documents from before A.D. 313 written by Christians, and they all say the same thing: that all Christians have always believed that Jesus is divine.

In fact, the historical sources prove that belief in Christ's divinity and Resurrection were part of Christianity even before the four Gospels were written, for this teaching is clear and central in Paul's Epistles (letters), and these were written before Paul died, which was between A.D. 55 and 59. They were probably written before the Gospels. The first creedal formula, "Jesus is Lord (*kyrios*, God)", is found in Paul's letters (1 Cor 12:3; Phil 2:11). So is the doctrine of the literal, bodily Resurrection of Jesus (1 Cor 15). Look at the data!

8. *It still doesn't make sense to believe that (a) Jesus is God, and (b) Jesus' Father is God, but (c) Jesus is not the same person as His Father. There's a logical contradiction there. And all three of these ideas are part of Christianity and are taught in the New Testament.*

They are. But there is not a contradiction there.

There's only one way to get all three of these divinely revealed truths together without contradiction, and that's the doctrine of the Trinity. The New Testament gives us the data, and the theological doctrine of the Trinity is the only explanation that accounts for all the data.

(Theology is like science that way: it has data, and its hypotheses are tested by its data. It's not like science in other ways: the data do not appear to our senses, and they can't be tested in laboratories.)

Here are the divinely revealed data for the doctrine of the Trinity:

a. There is only one God.

b. The Father is God. (Jesus says so.)

c. The Son is God. (Jesus says so.)

d. The Holy Spirit is God. (Jesus says so.)

e. Jesus is not the Father. He prays *to* the Father, and He conforms His will *to* the will of the Father ("not my will, but thine, be done" [Lk 22:42]). He says, "I seek not my own will but the will of him who sent me" (Jn 5:30). He says, "I do not seek my own glory" (Jn 8:50). He says, "My teaching is not mine, but his who sent me" (Jn 7:16).

f. Jesus is not the Holy Spirit. He promises that He will send the Spirit only after He leaves (Jn 16:7).

g. The Holy Spirit is not the Father, but the Father sends

Him (Gal 4:6; 1 Pet 1:12). (He is sent by both the Father and the Son.)

The only hypothesis that accounts for all seven pieces of the data (to use scientific language) is the doctrine of the Trinity: that the one God is three divine Persons, Father, Son, and Holy Spirit. God is one in nature and three in Persons. Jesus is one in Person and two in nature (divine and human).

That is not a logical contradiction. The idea that God is only one Person *and* is three Persons would be a logical contradiction. But that is not Christianity. And the idea that God has only one nature *and* has three natures would be a contradiction. But that is not Christianity. And the idea that God is one God with one nature in three Persons is *not* a contradiction. And that is Christianity.

The idea that Jesus is only one Person *and* is two Persons would be a logical contradiction. And the idea that Jesus has only one nature *and* has two natures would be a logical contradiction. But the idea that Jesus is only one Person but has two natures is not a logical contradiction. And that is Christianity.

It is not a contradiction, but it is a mystery. We cannot adequately understand it. Why should we expect adequately to understand it? What a ridiculous demand: that the creature adequately understand the Creator! We don't even understand our own souls very well; how could we expect to understand God? We don't even understand many things about the universe, that enormous collection of matter that doesn't have a rational soul; how could we claim to understand the soul? Most of us don't even understand the things we invented; how could we expect to understand the enormous universe God invented? As Woody Allen says in one of his movies, "My son wants to know 'If there is a God, why are there Nazis?' How should I know why there are Nazis? I don't even know how the can opener works."

9. *But even if the doctrine of the Trinity isn't a logical contradiction, it's not relevant to my life if I'm not a theologian. It's like Einstein's theory of relativity: it's not relevant to my life if I'm not a scientist.*

Nothing could be more relevant to your life than the doctrine of the Trinity. For life is meaningless to you unless you know life's meaning. And the meaning of life, the ultimate purpose of life, the greatest good, the supreme value, is love. And the doctrine of the Trinity is the foundation for that, because it means that love "goes all the way up" into ultimate reality, into the very essence of God. The doctrine of the Trinity means that God *is* love.

For if God is only one Person, not three, then God cannot *be* love; He can be only a *lover.* For love is a relationship between two persons. There have to be two persons for there to be love. So if God were only one Person, He could not love anyone else until that person existed, until He created him. He could love only Himself. He could have only selfish love, not unselfish love. He could not love the other until there *is* an other. And that other would have to be a creature, because there is no other God, only one. So if God were only one Person, then God would be dependent on us created persons in order to be a lover.

But if God is a Trinity, then from all eternity God *is* love, for God has an Other to love always: the other is within Himself. The Father eternally loves the Son, and the Son eternally loves the Father, and the Spirit of love proceeds from them both, eternally and spiritually, as a child proceeds from the love of a man and a woman temporally and materially, in time and in bodies. (Sex is an image of God, the Trinity of love. That's why sex is holy. See chapter X.)

Everyone loves the doctrine "God is love." Not everyone loves the doctrine of the Trinity. But the two go together. "God is love" depends on "God is a Trinity."

So to see the relevance of the doctrine of the Trinity to your life, we assume two things:

    a. Love is the highest meaning of life, and
    b. God is real, God is the ultimate reality and the Creator of everything real.

If God is not a Trinity, then God is not love. And if God is not love, then love is not the ultimate reality. And if love is not the ultimate reality, if love is not the really "real thing", then the highest meaning of life doesn't "go all the way up". The greatest reality (God) and the greatest good (love) do not coincide. And that would be the greatest tragedy.

So nothing could be more relevant to your life than the truth of the Trinity. Because the Trinity means that God is love, and therefore love is real, because God is real.

10. But all this still seems far away in Heaven, in eternity. What's the connecting link between God in eternity and my life here on earth Monday morning in my room?

Jesus is the connection. When He became a man, God reached down to earth, to you, to your life, to your room, to Monday morning. You touch God when you touch Jesus.

And you touch Jesus when you receive the Eucharist. That's not bread; that's Jesus!

He's alive. He didn't just rise from the dead two thousand years ago, in the past. He *is risen*, now, in the present. Bibles and churches should come with warning labels saying: "Look out! It's alive!" (Or "Aslan is not a *tame* lion.") He really gets *into* you. He *does things* to you. He changes you.

He's right here, inside your soul now, at this moment, doing things to you whenever you think of Him, and whenever you pray, and whenever you love. That's His Spirit helping you to love whenever you love. That's where love comes from.

When life gets really rough, you need more than good ideas and good ideals. You need a real friend to be with you and to stay with you, a friend who knows you better than you know yourself, who loves you better than you love yourself, and who has more power to help you than you have to help yourself. You need a God who is really present. You need a God who is real, not just an ideal.

That's exactly who Jesus is—and who He wants to be for you.

VII

Why be a Catholic?

1. If I had been brought up as a Hindu, I would have been a Hindu. If I had been brought up as a Muslim, I would have been a Muslim. So the only reason I'm a Catholic is because I've been brought up as a Catholic.

And if you had been brought up as a Nazi, you would have been a Nazi today. If that's your only reason for being a Catholic—that you were brought up that way—then you need this book very badly. You need to have better reasons than that. You need to be able to "be prepared to make a defense to any one who calls you to account for the hope that is in you" (1 Pet 3:15).

The way you were brought up is a psychological *cause* of those beliefs being in your mind now. Your teachers gave you those ideas. But you also need a logical *reason* for believing those ideas to be true.

Suppose I believe that all large black dogs are trying to kill me because a large black dog bit me when I was three, and the memory of that trauma still haunts me and prevents me from thinking reasonably about large black dogs. That's the *cause* of my believing that all large black dogs are trying to kill me, but that's not a good *reason* for believing it. It's only subjective, not objective; it's only a feeling, not a fact; it's only in me, not in the real world.

Believing a thing just because you have been brought up

that way, believing a thing just because your parents and your family believe it, is a very reasonable thing for a small child to do. When you were a small child, you were not able to think things through for yourself, and you had to trust your parents blindly—for instance, when your mother told you not to put your hand on the stove when the burner was on even though that burner didn't look hot to you, or when she warned you not to jump off the roof of the house even though you may have thought you could fly like a bird. That blind trust was a very reasonable thing for a small child. But now your trust needs to be less blind. You need to have more reasons, because you are becoming more able to think for yourself.

The *reasons* for believing the Catholic religion are essentially these three steps:

a. God is real.
b. God became a man in Jesus Christ.
c. Jesus Christ established the one visible Catholic Church to teach the whole world.

We believe what the Catholic Church teaches because it was given to us by Jesus, and we believe in Jesus because He was given to us by God the Father, and we believe in God because God is real.

We've looked at the reasons for believing God is real in chapter IV.

We've looked at the reasons for believing Jesus is God in chapter VI.

We're now ready to look at the reasons for believing that the Catholic Church is the Church Jesus established.

2. *It seems so narrow-minded to believe that the Catholic religion is the one true religion. Doesn't every person believe that his religion is the true one?*

Of course. If Muslims didn't believe that Islam was true, they wouldn't be Muslims. If Buddhists didn't believe that Buddhism was true, they wouldn't be Buddhists. If a person didn't believe that a certain religion was true, then that person would not believe it. That's what believing *means*: believing it to be true!

But if two beliefs contradict each other, one must be wrong.

Atheism says there is no God, and theism says there is. One of the two must be wrong.

Polytheism says there are many gods, and monotheism says there is only one God. One of the two must be wrong.

Some religions—Judaism and Christianity and Islam—believe that God created the universe. Other religions—Hinduism and Buddhism—do not. One of the two must be wrong.

Jews and Muslims believe Jesus was only a human being. Christians believe He was (and is) God. One of the two must be wrong.

Some Christians—Protestants—do not believe that Jesus established one visible Catholic Church and gave her His authority to teach all people for all time. Other Christians—Catholics—do believe that. One of the two must be wrong.

It's not narrow-minded to believe that others are wrong about some things. It is narrow-minded to believe that others are wrong about *everything*, that no one else knows any important truths at all. And it's also narrow-minded to believe that people who believe different things than you do are stupid people.

But to believe that an idea is either true or false is not narrow-mindedness; it's just clear, logical thinking. Different religions contradict each other about some important things. They can't all be right about everything.

No one believes that two ideas that contradict each other are both true *anywhere else*. Why believe that about religion? For instance, you wouldn't believe the idea that the earth is round and the idea that it isn't round. Or that I'm not plotting to murder you now and that I am. Or that the brain needs oxygen to live and that it doesn't. Whenever you're dealing with anything real, you always believe in the basic logical law of non-contradiction. Two contradictory ideas about anything real can't both be true.

But when you're dealing with something that's *not* real, then contradictory ideas can both be true. For instance, take elves. Elves are short and cute, not tall and awesome; *and* elves are tall and awesome, not short and cute. They're short and cute in Shakespeare's *Midsummer Night's Dream*, and they're tall and awesome in Tolkien's *Lord of the Rings*, because both are fiction, not fact. Elves aren't real.

So if you believe that different religions can be true even when they contradict each other, you're really saying that religions aren't real but fictions, like elves. When you say that all religions are true, you are really saying that they're all false! You're saying that God is not real but only in our minds, like elves. Whenever we deal with reality, we believe in the law of non-contradiction.

Of course, we might make mistakes about whether two religions really do contradict each other or not. For instance, we might think that Judaism and Christianity contradict each other about law and love because Judaism believes in law and Christianity believes in love; but that's a mistake because

Judaism believes in love too, and Christianity believes in law too.

Or we might think that Protestantism and Catholicism contradict each other on how to be saved because Protestants say we are saved by faith alone while Catholics say we are saved by faith and good works; but that's probably a mistake because when Protestants speak of being "saved", they mean only "getting to Heaven" (the theological term for this is "justification"), and when Catholics speak of being "saved", they mean also becoming a saint (the theological term for this is "sanctification"). You don't get to Heaven by piling up enough good works but by faith in Jesus the Savior. But without good works you can't become holy, or wholly good, which is what you must become when Jesus saves you. Jesus does not just save you from eternal *punishment* for your sins but from your *sins themselves.* "You shall call his name Jesus, for he will save his people from their sins" (Mt 1:21).

So we might think that two religions contradict each other on some questions when they really don't.

But Jews and Christians really do contradict each other on whether Jesus is God or not, and Catholics and Protestants really do contradict each other on whether or not the Catholic Church speaks with the authority of Jesus Christ and not just human authority.

No one can believe everything that all the religions of the world believe at the same time. You have to choose.

And you have to have good reasons to choose (1 Pet 3:15). That's why you need a book like this.

Christianity is not the only religion that has any truth, goodness, or beauty. The Church advises us to study other religions because we can find many great truths and much goodness and beauty there. But Christ is the source of all truth, goodness, and beauty, wherever it is to be found. He said, "I am the light of the world" (Jn 8:12), not just of Christians. He is "the true light that enlightens every man" (Jn 1:9).

This is often called "exclusivism". But the "exclusive" claim is not for the Christian religion but for Christ. Christianity is not the only religion that has any truth, but Christ is the only man who is God. Christianity is not the only religion that can make you a good person, but Christ is the only one who can save you. Christianity is not the only religion that can bring you joy in this life, but Christ is the only one who can bring you the fullness of eternal joy that we all long for, for He alone is God and brings us God in bringing us Himself. In the words of James Taylor's "New Hymn", "we hunt His face" in everything that we love. How do we find His face? The answer is Christ. Christ is the face of God and the essence of Christianity.

3. *If Christ is the only Savior, does that mean Christians are the only ones who are saved? That we won't find any Muslims or Buddhists in Heaven?*

No, it doesn't mean that.

Christ *is* the only Savior. He told us that (Jn 14:6). But He did not tell us how many people He saves. When His disciples asked Him, "Lord, will many be saved?" He replied neither "yes" nor "no" but "Strive to enter in" (Lk 13:24). We don't need to know the answer to the question about the comparative population statistics of Heaven and Hell. But we do need to know the answer to the question of how to get to Heaven, the question "What must I do to be saved?" (Acts 16:30). And Jesus is the answer to that question. (See the next verse, Acts 16:31: "Believe in the Lord Jesus, and you will be saved.")

"And there is salvation in no one else, for there is no other name under heaven given among men by which we must be saved" (Acts 4:12). This does not mean that only people who call themselves Christians can be saved; it means that when anyone is saved, it is by Christ.

Here is an analogy. A heart surgeon is the only person who can perform heart surgery. But that does not mean that only those who know their surgeon by name can receive his surgery. Jesus is the only one who can save your soul. But that does not mean that only Christians, who know their Savior by name, can be saved.

(But everyone *should* know—and love and thank—the Savior, just as you should know—and love and thank—the surgeon or fireman or policeman who saved your life.)

And our analogy between salvation and surgery also means that salvation must be voluntary, as surgery is. You have to consent to the operation. You have to ask for it; you have to choose it freely. You also have to consent to God's operation of salvation: you have to "repent and believe", repent of sin and believe God's offer of salvation. But non-Christians can do that even if they are quite confused about it, just as you can accept the gift of an operation on your heart and be healed, even if you are quite confused about who your surgeon is.

You don't get to Heaven by passing a theology test. You don't get there by doing enough good deeds either. (How many would be enough?) You get to Heaven by accepting God's offer of grace. No one knows just how much you have to *understand* with your mind in order to accept God with your heart or your will. So no one knows how many people will get to Heaven.

There will probably be many good, God-seeking Muslims and Buddhists and Jews and Hindus in Heaven. But Jesus alone can get them there. And they will know Him there much more truly than they knew Him here. And so will we!

4. Why be a Christian then? Why believe Christianity if non-Christians can be saved too?

Because Christianity is true! That's the only honest reason for believing anything.

5. How can there be so much truth and goodness and beauty in other religions if they were not founded by Christ, as Christianity was?

Because Christ is very generous and reveals some aspects of Himself to everyone. Saint John describes Him, in his Gospel, as "the true light that enlightens every man" (Jn 1:9). When a Muslim knows he must totally "surrender" (that is what "islam" means) to the one God, and fight a holy war, or "inner struggle" (that is one meaning of "jihad") against evil in his own soul, that is really Jesus enlightening his mind, though he does not know it. When a Buddhist knows he must give up all selfish desire and seek perfect peace, that is Jesus enlightening his mind, though he does not know it. When a Confucian knows he must practice moral virtue and live in harmony with his family and his community, that is Jesus enlightening his mind, though he does not know it.

6. People are different. Why should there be only one true religion? There are many roads to God, many paths up the same mountain.

People *are* different. And who can understand them all? Who can know what makes them all happy? Only the one God who created them all. That's why there is only one totally true religion: because there's only one totally true God, because God is real.

There *are* many paths up the mountain. But none of them can reach the top. We can't get to God and to Heaven by our own power. We are like ants trying to climb Mount Everest. But God in His mercy has made a road down the mountain to us. That road is Jesus. God has sent a helicopter to take us to the top of the mountain. That helicopter is Jesus.

He Himself says, "I am the way, and the truth, and the life; no one comes to the Father but by me" (Jn 14:6).

7. *But we shouldn't be judgmental.*

We *have* to be "judgmental" about geography, about which road leads home when we are lost in the dark. We have to be "judgmental" about chemistry, about what fuel will work in a car or a rocket ship. We have to be "judgmental" about the law, about who is guilty of committing a murder and who is innocent. We have to be "judgmental" about things that are real. And God is real. We have to be sure that we know and trust and worship and obey the true God, not a God of our own imagination. We're dealing with reality here!

Of course we should not be "judgmental" about people's hearts. Only God can judge people's hearts. What is present in a person's heart is subjective, internal, hidden, and private. But Christianity is objective, external, revealed, and public. We did not make it up; God did.

If you do not believe that, if you believe we made it all up, if you believe that God is an invention or projection of the human imagination, then when you worship God you are really worshipping yourself, worshipping the work of your own imagination. That is idolatry. An idol that is made of ideas is just as much an idol as an idol that is made of stone or wood. Both the idea and the stone or wooden statue are man-made. To worship what is man-made is to worship a false God, not the true God. That is a very serious sin. It is a violation of the first and most basic of the Ten Commandments. It is idol worship. And worshipping your own ideas is the worst kind of idol worship, for it is worshipping yourself.

8. *But there are other forms of Christianity too. Why be a Catholic? What does the Catholic Church have that no Protestant church has? Isn't it true that there are many very good and holy people in Protestant churches, and many wicked people in the Catholic Church?*

Of course that's true. There are good and bad people everywhere. The right reason for being a Catholic is not to find the nicest people but to obey and follow Christ. And Christ established the Catholic Church.

Protestants too accept the New Testament as God's revelation. But the New Testament tells us that Christ established one single visible Church and gave His apostles the authority to teach in His name (Lk 10:16).

The Nicene Creed, the fourth-century creed that we recite at Mass every Sunday, lists four "marks of the Church". They are "one, holy, Catholic, *and apostolic*". And the only church that has "apostolic succession" is the Catholic Church. The New Testament tells us that Christ authorized His apostles and that these apostles authorized successors, "bishops" to carry on this authority. The Pope and bishops of the Catholic Church are the only ones in the world who can trace their teaching authority ("magisterium") back to the apostles and thus back to Christ.

9. So what do Catholics have that other Christians don't have?

The Catholic Church has

a. The authority to teach in Christ's name;

b. The literal, full, total, real presence of Jesus Christ in the Eucharist;

c. The power of the priest to change bread and wine into the Body and Blood of Christ;

d. The power of the priest to forgive your sins, in the confessional, in the name of Jesus Christ. "If you forgive the sins of any, they are forgiven; if you retain the sins of any, they are retained" (Jn 20:23) are Jesus' words to His apostles, and the successors they appointed; and

e. The infallibility of the public teaching authority of the Church, the guarantee that God will not lead His Church into error but only into truth (Jn 16:13) when she teaches in His name, invoking apostolic authority.

It is a historical fact that for two thousand years, there has been only one Church that has never officially taught error, never contradicted herself, never changed her teaching. No matter how wicked or stupid the teachers were, they never changed the teaching. God preserved them from that. The Church has *developed* her teaching, as your body has developed, but never changed it. It has grown but never shrunk. The Church has made many practical and pastoral mistakes, and she repented of them, but she never "repented" of any of her doctrines.

It is true that some Catholics have been very wicked, and some Protestants have been very holy. But we can't choose what church to belong to by judging which one has fewer sinners in it. In the first place, we can't judge how saintly and how sinful people are. *That's* being judgmental. That's "playing God". And in the second place, the Church isn't supposed to be a museum for saints but a hospital for sinners. Of course there are going to be a lot of sick people in a hospital; that's what a hospital is for. Of course there are going to be a lot of wicked, sinful people in Christ's Church; that's what he established the Church for. "I came not to call the righteous, but sinners" (Mt 9:13).

The Church is like your family: she's far from perfect, and she's often pretty messed up, but she's *real*. Because God is real.

10. *Can you summarize the reasons for being a Catholic?*

Yes: Because Catholicism is true, and good, and beautiful.

The first reason is that it's *true*. It's just not honest to believe any religion if it isn't true. It's not honest to believe *anything* if is isn't true. Catholic Christianity is true because it's the revelation of God's mind, it's God way to think, it is "the mind of Christ" (Phil 2:5; 1 Cor 2:16).

The second reason is that it's *good*. It shows us the way to goodness, virtue, holiness, saintliness. Catholic Christianity is good because it teaches God's law, the revelation of God's will.

The third reason is that it's *beautiful*. It brings us joy. It's the astonishing and dramatic "good news" that the Creator, the eternal, perfect, all-powerful Ultimate Reality, is in love with each one of us and has destined us for the eternal ecstasy of spiritual marriage forever to the infinitely beautiful Creator and inventor of everything in the universe that is beautiful and joyful, from stars and seas to sex and babies. Catholic Christianity is beautiful because it is the revelation of God's heart.

The truths are the theology, summarized in the creeds.

The goods are the morality, summarized in the Commandments.

The beauty is the prayer and worship, summarized in the Lord's Prayer and the Mass.

Everything else is unfolded and unpacked from these three.

VIII

Why go to Church?

1. Not many people are "turned off" by the idea of God. But many are "turned off" by the Church. Most people are not "turned off" by the idea of a church. Why is that?

Because the Church is concrete, like your mother. The *idea* of "mother" is beautiful, and you never had fights or misunderstandings with the idea of "mother"; but you have had fights and misunderstandings with your actual mother. The idea of an "ark of safety and salvation from the flood" is a beautiful idea, but if you found yourself on Noah's actual, particular ark, you would have a lot to complain about as you were arguing about who had to mop up the elephant poop! Well, the Church is like the ark, and we are like the animals. The important thing about the ark is that it *works*. It does its work, as a hospital does its work.

2. What work does the Church do? Why does she have to exist? It doesn't seem as practical and necessary as a hospital, or an ark in a flood.

The work of the Church is even more necessary and more practical than the work of a hospital. The work of the Church is to save souls, as a hospital's work is to save bodies. The Church exists to change sinners into saints. To put it in a crude metaphor, the Church is a saint-making machine. She's like a big confessional booth: Adam walks in and Jesus walks out.

Only God can do that, of course. But He uses the Church as His instrument to get through to us. He gets His mind through to us through the creeds. He gets His will through to us through the Commandments. And He gets His very life, His grace, His power, through to us through the sacraments.

3. Why do I have to go to Church every Sunday? It doesn't turn me on.

First of all, "turning you on" is not the essential purpose of the Mass. It's not a movie or a concert. It's more like food. Spinach probably doesn't "turn you on" either, but it works. It makes you strong.

Second, there are three reasons to go to Church. These three reasons correspond to the three Persons of the Trinity.

First, we go to Church to worship God because God is real and really deserves to be worshipped. He is our infinitely wise and powerful Creator, our infinitely good and loving Father, and our infinitely beautiful and joyful eternal destiny.

Second, we go to Church to worship God because God is not only real but also really *there*, really present there. God the Son, Jesus Christ, is really, literally, present in the Eucharist.

Third, we go to Church to worship God because God really inspires us there. It is His Holy Spirit who moves us to worship Him and to love Him and to love each other. The Holy Spirit is the "soul of the Church", as your soul is the soul of your body.

It's very simple: we go to Church to meet God. If we love God, we will want to meet Him wherever He is. Of course He is everywhere, and we can meet Him everywhere. But He is in Church too, waiting for us. And through His Church He calls us to come there on Sundays and Holy Days.

4. *Can't you be saved without going to Church?*

Yes. God can work outside His sacraments too. But He gave us His Church and His sacraments to use. There is no good reason not to use them. And if we know that He requires us to go to Church and we choose not to go despite that, and if we don't repent, then we can't be saved because we are deliberately refusing to do His will.

"Outside the Church there is no salvation" is a formula from the early Church Fathers. It does not mean that only Catholics can be saved. It means that (a) when anyone is saved, he is saved by Christ, even if perhaps he does not know who He is; and (b) he is saved by being made into part of Christ's Body; and (c) Christ's Body is the Church; and (d) the Catholic Church is Christ's Church in her fullness. Non-Catholics can also be saved; Christ can make them into parts of His Body too even though non-Catholics do not have the *fullness* of His Body that Catholics have, for instance all the creeds, all the sacraments, and all the teaching authority ("magisterium").

Of course we are not saved just because we go to Church each Sunday. But going to Church is deeply connected with our salvation, for we go to Church each Sunday to worship Jesus our Savior, to offer Him up to the Father in the Mass for the salvation of the world, and actually to receive our Savior into our bodies and souls in the Eucharist.

There are other good reasons for going to Church, such as "celebration" and "community" and "sharing", but they are not the main reason, because we can do all those things else-where too. We don't go to Church merely to meet each other; we go to Church to meet God, because God is real, as real as we are, and God is really present there, as really present as we are.

God is also present elsewhere, but not as fully, literally, and objectively present as He is in the Mass. He makes Himself subjectively present to our souls in many places outside the Church. He can be present to us in a forest, but we don't wor-ship a tree. He can be present to us when a baby is born, but we don't call the baby our Savior. He can be present to us through inspired music or art, but the music or art that God inspired is not the God who inspired it.

5. Why do we need the Church's sacraments?

We are saved by Christ. Christ actually changes us, transforms our life into His life. But how? How does Christ get His sal-vation and His life into us?

Through the sacraments.

A sacrament is a sacred sign, instituted by Christ, that actually ef-fects what it signifies. That means that it does what it says, it performs what it points to—like the words "I love you" or "I, King Arthur, hereby dub thee a Knight of the Round Table."

What do all the sacraments point to? To the God who is real and who is really giving grace to our souls as we receive the sacraments. The sacraments bring God's grace (God's gifts, God's love, God's very life) into our souls. They bring God down from Heaven to earth just as really as rain brings water down from the heavens to the earth.

There are seven sacraments: Baptism, Eucharist, Confirmation, Confession, Ordination, Marriage, and Anointing of the Sick (or the Sacrament of the Sick).

When you are baptized, the very life of Christ begins in you.

When you receive the Eucharist, you literally receive Christ.

When you receive Confirmation, that life is strengthened and matured in you.

When you confess your sins, it is Christ who takes them away.

If you are ordained a priest, the real power to change bread and wine into Christ's Body and Blood is given to you.

If you get married, God actually gives you the power to give the whole of yourself in love to your spouse, as God gives the whole of Himself to you.

If you are anointed with the Sacrament of the Sick, you are actually empowered spiritually—and sometimes even physically—to conquer disease and death.

A house usually has at least seven rooms. They correspond to seven aspects of life. They also correspond to the seven sacraments.

The hallway is the first room you enter when you enter a house. That is like Baptism.

The living room is where your life together as a family is strengthened and matured. That is like Confirmation, which means to "make firm" (*firmo*) "together with" (*con*).

The bathroom is where you get rid of your dirt. That is like Confession.

The kitchen is where you cook your food. That is like Ordination, which creates the priests who "confect" the Eucharist.

The dining room is where you eat your "daily bread". That is like the Eucharist.

The bedroom contains the *marriage* bed.

And a sick room is where you are given medicine when you are ill. That is like Anointing of the Sick.

The seven basic rooms of a house provide for the seven basic aspects of physical life, and the seven sacraments of the Church provide for the seven basic aspects of our spiritual life.

We receive God's grace only through Christ. But we do not receive Christ's life *only* through the sacraments. God also works outside His sacraments.

But that does not mean you can neglect them, for they are the ways He Himself has instituted" (invented) to connect Himself to you; to connect you to God and God to you. The sacraments are like tubes that actually put the Christ-life into us, like a blood transfusion. On one hand, that's not a very good image because it is too crude and physical. On the other hand, it *is* a good image because the blood you receive through a tube is *real*, and the grace you receive through the sacraments is just as real as that blood, even though it is invisible and spiritual, not visible and material. Though God's grace is not a material thing, it comes to us *through* material things, just as our love for each other is not a material thing but we communicate it to each other through material things like words, deed, gifts, hugs, and kisses. The sacraments are like God's hugs and kisses.

The sacraments are not magic because magic is like a machine that works whether you want it to or not. Once you push the button, the Coke machine simply delivers the Coke, and once the princess touches the frog with her magic wand, the frog turns into a prince. Of course, there are no real magic wands, as there are real Coke machines; the point is just that magic and technology work the same way: automatically. But the sacraments, even though they are what they are independent of us, do not work automatically; they work in proportion to your faith. You have to believe in them and want them. They are like kisses, not slaps. God freely gives them *and we freely receive them*. They are not transactions between a person and an unfree machine; they are transactions between two free persons, you and God. He freely gives you Himself in these gifts, and you freely accept Him in receiving them. For something to be a gift, it must be freely given and freely received.

You can't start sacraments up by your own faith and hope and love, but you can shut them down by your lack of faith and hope and love. God's grace is like water. The sacraments are like a hose. Our faith, hope, and love are like a faucet handle. It's up to us how far to turn the handle. The more faith we have, the more of God's grace gets through. But that grace is not *caused* by our faith.

God packages Himself in the sacraments, so to speak. He puts Himself into these material boxes and wraps them up and gives Himself to us in these presents, these gifts of grace. ("Grace" means "undeserved gift".) He does this to "get through" to us. For He designed us to be material as well as spiritual creatures, so He gives Himself to us in material as well as spiritual ways. He's a pure spirit, not a body, but we are bodies as well as spirits, so He makes connection with us in bodily ways as well as spiritual ways.

Of course He is outside these "packages" as well as inside them. He is not confined or limited to them.

*6. My church is in my heart. I need no externals, no crutches.
Organized religion is a crutch.*

If you really believe that, you're in trouble. You're proud. You
think your heart is enough. But it is not. Your heart is not
perfect, any more than your body is. It needs help; it needs a
"crutch". Religion is indeed a crutch: we are all cripples. Don't
you know yourself well enough to know that?

You need externals everywhere else in your life, even in the
most important things, even in love. If someone loves you, you
want to hear the external words "I love you", and you want
to see the external deeds of love. You don't receive beauty
only spiritually; you receive it physically: it's not the *idea* of
great music but the physical sounds that you want to hear.
Even ideas have to be communicated and received physically,
through words, in print (visibly) or in sound vibrations (audi-
bly).

You're not safe from evil if you try to take refuge in spirit, in
"spirituality". The most evil and dangerous being in all reality is a pure spirit. He's called the Devil. Matter, on the other
hand, is innocent and even holy, for

a. God created all of it and pronounced it "good" (Gen
1:31);

b. God incarnated Himself in it, in the human body of
Christ;

c. Jesus died physically to save us. He did not save us by
merely teaching good ideas but by dying on the Cross. He
saved us by giving us His Blood, not by giving us His philosophy (though He did that too). When He gave Himself to
us in the Eucharist, He did not say "This is my mind" but
"This is my body" (1 Cor 11:24);

d. Jesus did not take off His human body when He ascended back to Heaven but took it with Him forever; and

e. Jesus comes to us now in a physical way in the sacraments, especially in the Eucharist.

7. *The Church is just an authority figure, like a bossy teacher. That's what the Church is really all about: power.*

No, it isn't. The Church is a mother as well as a teacher. ("Mater et magistra", "mother and teacher", is what the Church calls herself.) And the "mother" aspect comes first, before the "teacher" aspect. The Church is like both Mary (the mother) and Peter (the Rock—"Peter" means "rock"), but more like Mary, first like Mary, primarily like Mary. (Pope John Paul II said "the Marian dimension of the Church is prior to the Petrine one.") Thus the Church is always called "she", not "he". Like a mother, she brings forth life; she gives us spiritual life as a mother gives her babies physical life, and she nourishes that life as a nursing mother nourishes her baby. Whether we are male or female, we all began our life in this world from our mother's womb. Then, secondly, the Church is also the Rock of Peter, the strong man, the warrior who defends the faith by teaching it and defining it and clarifying it.

The Church teaches with Christ's authority. But "authority" does not mean "power". "Authority" is not "might" but "right". The world's concept of authority is that "might makes right"; the Christian concept of authority is that "right makes might". The word "authority" contains the word "author". "Authority" means "author's rights". God is the author of our very being; He is our Creator. That's why He has authority:

not because He has the might (though He does) but because He has the right.

And instead of exercising His right to rule over us directly, He has given authority to human intermediaries, He has chosen to rule us through human means: popes and bishops and priests—and parents, and civil rulers, whether kings and queens or parliaments and congresses.

These "rulers" are all our servants, not our masters. Christ made that clear when He washed His disciples' feet and said that that was how His authority was supposed to be exercised by them: in service. It's a radical change from the world's notion of authority as power.

That includes a husband's "authority" or "headship" over his wife: its model is not a boss' authority over his business or a general's authority over his troops but Christ's authority over His Church: "For the husband is the head of the wife as Christ is the head of the church, his body. . . . Husbands, love your wives, as Christ loved the church and gave himself up for her. . . . Husbands should love their wives as their own bodies. He who loves his wife loves himself. For no man ever hates his own flesh, but nourishes and cherishes it, as Christ does the church, because we are members of his body" (Eph 5:23, 25, 28–30).

So if you say silly things like "The Church is a power structure" or "Women should be priests because they should share the power", that shows how deeply you are misunderstanding the whole purpose of the Church, and of Christ. You are thinking like the world, not like Christ. His Church is not all about power. She's all about love. And that means service and self-giving and sacrifice and salvation. That's what love does.

8. The Church is hung up on the past and tradition. She looks back at a man who died two thousand years ago. She should be looking at the real world of the present.

That man who died two thousand years ago is not dead. He rose. And He is as "now" as you are, as really present today as you are.

How is He present now? Well, let's look at how *we* are present here and now. We are present here and now by our bodies. We may be "absent-minded", but we are never "absent-bodied". We may be *thinking* about other places or other times, but we are really present here and now even when we think about there and then. You are wherever your body is. So it is with Christ. And the Body of Christ is the Church. So it is by His Church that He is present here and now.

It is the Church that brings Christ across the centuries, across the gaps of place and time, from Jerusalem in A.D. 33 to Manayunk, Pennsylvania in A.D. 2008. Christ is more up to date than today's newspaper. And it is the Church that does that "progressive" thing, that brings Christ to us in the present.

The two main ways the Church "presents" Christ, or makes Him present, are by Word and by sacrament: (a) by preaching His Gospel and applying it to modern problems, and (b) by making not just His teachings but Jesus Himself really present, in person, in the Mass. At Mass, the sacrifice of Christ on the Cross two thousand years ago is made really present and is offered to the Father for our eternal future, for our salvation. The Mass does not only *remember* Christ but makes Him really present. The Mass is not nostalgia for the past; it's power for the present so as to save the future, not just humanity's future time on earth but our eternal future in Heaven. Christ is not just our super social worker; He is our Savior.

9. *I just don't get anything out of it when I go to Church. What should I do?*

If you give something to it, you will get something out of it.

What do you have to give to it? First of all, faith. If you really believe it, if you believe what the Church teaches, then you will get something out of it.

What will you get out of it? You will get God's grace out of it. Grace is soul food.

The Church is not a feel-good pop psychologist. You don't have to "*feel* it" to "get it". You don't feel the power of a medicine, either, but you do really get something out of it. You get real healing.

Feeling is the effect, not the cause. You *will* feel it; you will feel God's peace and happiness and joy. But that's not the first reason why you go to Church. Those feelings are the "extras".

You will experience the extras only if you let God speak to your soul. But to do that, you have to be open and silent and receptive. Stop fretting and chattering. Ignore the clock. Turn off the noise. Enter the holy silence. Go into a church or chapel sometime when it's empty and quiet and just be alone with Him. Look at the crucifix. Look how He spreads His arms on that Cross to embrace the whole world. Look at the God who is *that* real. Listen to the "good news" of how much He loves you and then tell Him you love Him back. He's waiting for you.

10. *That's private devotion, not public liturgy. Okay, then religion should be private, and inward, and invisible, and purely spiritual, not public, external, visible, and material.*

Not God's religion. The religion God gave us is both. It's for the whole human person, not just the soul and not just the body.

What God did to relate to us (that's what "religion" means fundamentally, "relationship") was not just private. Noah's ark was not private. The people God chose, the Jews, were not an invisible, private, secret society but a visible, identifiable people. Jesus Christ, God incarnate, was not an invisible spirit but a visible man who was physically born and killed and resurrected. His life was the most public life ever lived. And the Church He established is not a secret society of private spiritualists but a public, visible, identifiable institution. The Church of the martyrs was not a Church of good intentions but of public deeds.

You can't separate Christ from His Church because you can't separate Christ from His Body, and the Church is His greater Body. It is not His club or His business. He is the Church's "head", not her boss or CEO. We are members of the Church not as we are members of a club but as your eyes and ears are members of your body. You can't take the head and leave the body behind without cutting the head off the body, and that's the work of the guillotine. Head and body are one person.

The Church is a body, and a body is an organism, not just an organization. A body is not like a machine. It's alive, like an animal. With nonliving things like businesses or buildings, you can add new parts or take away parts without changing the thing. You can't do that to an organism, a living thing. You can't add a wing or subtract a wing from a bird as you can add or subtract a wing from a building.

In an organism, every organ (or "member") does a different work. Eyes and ears are not interchangeable. But in things that are not alive, the parts are interchangeable. You can rotate and change the tires on your car, but you can't rotate and change the arms and legs on your body.

Every single organ of an organism is unique. That's not so with nonliving things: any two dollar bills in a wallet, or any two bricks in a wall, are identical and replaceable. But in an organism, each organ is unique and necessary. Heart and brain, lung and kidney, eye and ear are each unique, for each do a unique work for the body that no other organ can do. But they do it for the whole body, not just for themselves.

The Church is a body, a spiritual organism. Every single member is different and essential. That means that your prayers and your worship are essential too. No one else can take your place. You need to be there in Church on Sunday because you an organ in Christ's body.

IX

Why be moral?

1. The word "morality" is not a word that turns most people on. Why should it?

Because it tells us about ourselves and the meaning of our lives.

Morality tells us not only about ourselves but also about God, because it tells us God's plan, God's will, for our lives. The Church's teaching is the revelation of God's mind and will, not just human minds and wills. Catholic morality does not come from the Church; it comes from God *through* the Church, just as Catholic theology does.

If we love truth, we must love the truth of Catholic theology; and if we love goodness, we must love the good of Catholic morality. Catholic morality *should* turn you on because living it will turn your life on, so to speak, just as following the directions for starting a car will turn the car on.

2. Morality does not turn most people on because morality is a set of rules, and rules restrict our freedom.

There are two very common mistakes here. First, morality is not merely a set of rules. Second, rules don't threaten freedom.

a. The essence of morality is not first of all a set of rules but a way of living, and that way *should* be a "turn-on" because it is the way of Christ and His saints, the way of love. All kinds of love, spiritual as well as physical, "turn us on". "Everybody loves a lover." You have to be very wicked to hate a saint.

True morality is a turn-on because it makes us deeply happy. And it also makes those around us happy, while morally wrong ways of living make us and others unhappy.

Of course morality has rules, but the rules are not *it*; they only define it and describe it, as a road map describes roads. Road maps give directions. The road map alone is not a turn-on, but the trip is. The rules for the good life are not a turn-on but the good life is.

A life of love is not boring. It is a drama. It is a love story, and also a war story, a battle of good against evil, of love against lovelessness. The rules are the directions for this great drama. Moral rules are battle plans for the great war.

Living is like traveling: our destination depends on which roads we choose. Different roads lead to different destinations. That is just as true of our moral choices as it is of our physical choices. Every choice makes a difference. In fact, each choice makes a difference to many lives, as a stone thrown into a pool makes ripples that touch every part of the pond.

b. Rules do not threaten freedom. Only bad rules threaten freedom, like the rules of a tyrant. Good rules are necessary *for* freedom. This is true of everything in life: music, math, sports. If you don't follow the rules of music, you don't make music, just noise. If you don't follow the rules of math, you don't find the right answers. If you don't play by the rules of basketball, you don't play basketball but something else.

Life without moral rules is not more free; it's less free. It's chaos. If the rules don't rule, then power rules. If right doesn't rule, then might rules. Bullies win. The strong take advantage of the weak. To see what life is like without rules, watch untrained babies or animals fighting. True morality is the *way* to freedom: freedom from tyrants and bullies, freedom from chaos and misery.

If God invented human beings, then His rules for human life are the right rules. If you want to know the right rules for operating a machine, ask the inventor of the machine. If you want to know the right rules for understanding a textbook, ask the author of the textbook. If you want to know the right rules for human life, ask the Author and inventor of human life. The Author has the author-ity.

3. *So morality comes from God. That sounds like "I'm God, and I'm the boss, so you have to do what I tell you." So moral goodness is really based on power. It's good only because the boss says so.*

No, it's not just that God is "the boss" and has the power to lay down the rules. They are not external rules, arbitrary rules, interference from outside. Rather, God put the rules *into our own nature* when He created us, just as He put the laws of physics into the very nature of matter when He created matter. Moral law is called the "natural law" because it is a law written in human nature, not just in books.

For instance, part of human nature is intelligence. We need to know things to fulfill that part of our nature. That's why the natural law forbids lying. Another part of human nature is free will. We need to make free choices to fulfill that power of our nature. That's why the natural law forbids forcing people to do your will against their will, by force and violence—for instance, aggressive war and slavery.

Another part of human nature is our material needs, such as food, and money to buy food. That's why the natural law commands us to feed the hungry and help the poor.

Another part of human nature is the need to own our own material things that we can work with. Otherwise we cannot do our own work and be proud of it. That's why the natural law forbids stealing.

Another part of human nature is the need for families to bring us into the world and bring us up; to help us grow physically, mentally, and morally; and to teach us to love, by example, by loving us. That's why the natural law commands love and respect and obedience to parents.

Families are created by marriage and preserved by faithfulness, by fidelity. That's why the natural law forbids adultery.

Human nature obviously needs physical bodies to be alive. That's why the natural law forbids murder.

Another part of human nature is the need to relax and take time off from work. That's one reason why the natural law commands a work-free Sabbath day.

Above all, human nature needs to receive its real good from the God who is real. That's why the first commandment forbids idolatry, worshipping gods who are not real.

An ancient Greek philosopher (Socrates) once asked: "Is a thing good because God wills it, or does God will it because it's good?" His answer was that God wills it because it's good. That is the right answer. God is not arbitrary. He designed our human nature, and His will is that we fulfill our own human nature. He wants us to obey His will *so that we can be fully human and happy.*

*4. How does God come into this, then, if morality is just the rules
for being human and happy? Do the rules come from human
nature or from God?*

The ultimate source of morality is God. We must be good
because God is good. God repeats over and over again to His
chosen people the reason for morality in the Old Testament:
"Be holy, for I am holy" (Lev 11:44). To be good is to be like
God.

God's law comes from God's will, and God's will comes from
His nature. He wills the moral law according to His nature.

The ultimate source and standard of morality is God's nature. But the proximate (immediate) source of morality is human nature, which God made "in His own image" (Gen 2:27).
It is not human *wills*, which change, but human *nature*, which
does not change, that is the standard of morality. That is why
the principles of morality do not change.

The connection between the ultimate standard of morality
(God's nature) and the proximate standard of morality (human
nature) is the fact that God created us in His own image. So
when we know and choose the good, we polish and perfect
His image in us as you would polish a diamond. Doing that
makes us more human *and* more like God.

And being more like God means being more real, because
God is real. The better you are, the more real you are.

5. *But morality is still a set of rules, laws. The Ten Command-ments are not "suggestions" or "values" or "ideals". God didn't give Moses the "ten good ideas".*

That's true. The Commandments are *laws*, not *suggestions*. There is no if, and, or but about them!

But the rules, laws, or commandments are not the final end, not the main point of human life, not the greatest good. We don't exist for the rules; the rules exist for us.

They are for us not only in the sense that they are given to us rather than to animals or angels or Martians, but also in the sense that they are for our benefit. They are like good servants: they exist for us; we do not exist for them. When Jesus was speaking about one of the Commandments, the one about the Sabbath, He said, "The sabbath was made for man, not man for the sabbath" (Mk 2:27).

The rules, laws, or commandments of morality are impor-tant not because they are ends in themselves but because they are the necessary means to a higher end. The end result of fol-lowing the rules is being a good person. Every time you make a morally right choice, you turn yourself into a better person. And the result of that is happiness. In other words, (a) you can't be good without following the rules (the real rules, the natural rules), and (b) you can't be really happy (truly happy, long-range happy, deep-down happy) without being good.

All the saints are happy. The better you are, the happier you are. And the more sinful you are, the more unhappy you are. That is simply a fact. The Devil's greatest lie is that being good makes you miserable and being bad makes you happy.

6. *How does being good make you happy? Goody-goody people who always obey the rules aren't happy. They're unintelligent and unimaginative and repressed.*

Being good doesn't mean being goody-goody. It means being morally intelligent, not stupid; morally imaginative, not unimaginative; and morally free, not bound. Being good is being *real*, being a "real woman" or a "real man"—being a *mensch*, to use a great, untranslatable Yiddish term.

It's the wicked person who's stupid. Like everyone else, he wants to be happy, but he doesn't know that moral goodness is the way to be happy. He's morally stupid, because he thinks he'll be happier if he fills his pockets with stolen money than if he fills his soul with moral goodness. He thinks his pockets are more important than his soul.

And it's the wicked person who's morally unimaginative. A wicked person could never imagine great stories about moral good and evil in human life, as Shakespeare and Dickens and Tolstoy and Tolkien did. And it's the wicked person who's unfree. He's addicted to his idols, his false gods and false goods, addicted to his money or pleasure or power, just as a drug addict is addicted to his drug. That's the opposite of freedom.

7. *Why be good at all? Why not be evil? Why not be a stupid, spoiled little brat? Why not be a snob? Why not be a selfish pig? What's so good about being good?*

To be good is to be real, to be really human, to be what you are, to be what a human being is supposed to be, to be a success at your life's most important task, being a human being. Don't get all A's but flunk Life.

There's a second reason for being good: to please God, who loved you into existence by creating you. He *deserves* your goodness.

And here is a third reason: being good, as we said above, is the only way to be happy. That's a well-known fact. The secret of happiness is no secret at all. You know it from experience. The secret of happiness is to practice the heart and center of morality, unselfish love; it is to forget yourself and love others. Not just "others" in general but your concrete, individual neighbors, the actual people you know and meet, your family and friends. Jesus never told us to "love others" or "love humanity" but to "love your neighbor as yourself."

If you try it, you'll like it. It is the most certain experiment in the world: whenever you do it, it works—you are happy. And whenever you don't do it, whenever you live like a selfish pig, you are unhappy. It's an infallible formula. It works every time.

If you have the slightest doubt about this, you can prove it to yourself simply by trying it, performing the experiment in the laboratory of your life. Everyone who has tried it—has really tried it—has discovered the same result.

There are two kinds of people in the world: givers and takers. Givers are happy. Takers are not. That is simply a fact.

Giving is what love does. And love is the secret of happiness. So the secret of happiness is to be a giver. The secret of being happy is to make others happy.

And that is a fourth reason to be good: it makes others happy, as well as yourself.

Making others happy and making yourself happy are not rivals, but they reinforce each other. Your happiness grows when you share it. Material goods diminish when we share them, but spiritual goods multiply when we share them. When we share our money or our food with others, we have less left ourselves. But when we share our knowledge or our love with others, we have *more* after we do that than we had to start with.

8. *Okay, so love is the heart of morality. So in the words of the old song, "Love is all you need." The rest of morality is a set of rules that restrict love.*

No, morality is the rules that protect love.

But what kind of love is this that is the essence of morality? Not just *falling* in love, but *rising* in love. Not just a passive *feeling* but an active *choice*.

Wonderful as it is, the feeling of falling in love is only a feeling. It is like a wave: it comes and goes. It is wonderful to surf on but impossible to build on. Love must have a secure and lasting foundation if we are to build the house of our lives on it. But what kind of love can that be? What is the essence of love?

The essence of love is to will the good of the other, as you will the good of yourself. Jesus defined it simply: "Love your neighbor as yourself." How do you love yourself? You don't always have the same feelings toward yourself. Sometimes you feel good about yourself, and sometimes you don't. But you always *will* good to yourself, even if you don't *feel* good about yourself.

That is how we are to love others. When Jesus commanded us to love, He could not possibly have meant the feeling of love, because feelings can't be commanded. What a fool I would be if I commanded you to have sweet, kind feelings toward me all the time! Jesus isn't commanding us what to feel but what to will, what to choose and what to do. Feelings don't obey rules because they are not under our control. They just arise in us without our will. We can control how we act and even how we think—we can direct our thoughts to one thing or another—but we cannot control how we feel.

(We can, however, encourage some feelings by directing our thoughts in one way and discourage other feelings by directing our thoughts in another way. The more you choose to think about someone or something that makes you feel angry, the angrier you feel. The more you *choose* to sneer at or scorn a person, the more you *feel* scorn for him. Our thoughts and actions can alter our feelings quite a bit, but they can't create feelings when they're not there, and they can't usually destroy feelings entirely once they are there.)

But though our feelings don't obey rules, our actions do. Rules are for the areas of life that are under our control, under our free choice. We can choose how we act, and the rules tell us how to choose and act rightly.

Love plays by the rules—the rules that are natural to it. For instance, when you love someone, (a) you put him first; (b) you don't use him as a tool, as a means to another end; (c) you do not insult him; (d) you take time to be with him; (e) you honor him and his family; (f) you respect his life; (g) you respect his property; (h) you respect his body; (i) you respect his mind: you do not lie to him; (j) you are content with him. This is what love does if it is true love. These are the ten commandments of love, the ten things that love naturally does when it is true to its own nature, when it is *real* love.

9. So how do you bridge the gap between law and love?

There is no gap. The moral laws, the Commandments, are the laws of love, the inner laws of love, the natural laws of love, the laws that describe the very nature of love, just as the rules of hygiene and diet and exercise are the inner, natural rules for bodily health.

The "ten things that love naturally does" that were mentioned above just happen to be the Ten Commandments of God in the Bible (Ex 20). To see this, let's look at each of the Ten Commandments from the perspective of love.

1. "You shall have no other gods before Me." That means no other "number one" in your life. That's a law of love. Love is faithful. Love puts the beloved first. Love does not worship idols.

2. "You shall not take the name of the Lord your God in vain." Love does not insult the name of the beloved. Love honors the beloved, praises the beloved, cherishes the name and reputation of the beloved. Love says: "Look! Sec how lovable my beloved is!" Love is a missionary, an evangelist. Love testifies, love preaches, love sings the praises of the beloved. Love does not insult the beloved.

3. "Remember the sabbath day, to keep it holy." Love takes sabbaticals. Love takes time from work to enjoy the company of the beloved. For time *is* life: it's your "lifetime". Love means sharing your life, and that means sharing your time. If you say you love someone yet don't want to spend time with him, you lie. If you love God, you will pray, not just once a day but many times. You will want to be with, and talk with, your Best Friend.

4. "Honor your father and your mother." Love honors and respects the family of the beloved, for they gave the beloved life! And love honors and respects the institution of the family itself, for love, when it matures, will create a new family when it marries.

Even nonmarried love, nonromantic loves, like friendship

and charity and kindness, give birth to spiritual children, in a way. Those children are: all the benefits given to all the people who will receive the love. For instance, priests, teachers, doctors, nurses, social workers, counselors, rulers, soldiers, lawyers—these are not just *jobs* but *vocations* (literally, "callings"). They are ways of responding to God's call to live by helping others. They are ways of loving.

5. "You shall not kill." This is obvious: if you love someone, you do not kill him.

Love says: "I am happy you exist." Killing says: "I am unhappy that you exist." Love respects life and defends life against all attacks against it. Love fights against all the little deaths as well as the final death. Love fights against disease, weakness, pain, and depression as well as death. Love always chooses life (Dt 30:19) and fights on the side of life against the forces of death.

6. "You shall not commit adultery." Love is unadulterated. Love is pure. Love is faithful. Love does not cheat. When love matures into marriage, love says: "I give the whole of myself to the whole of you. I do not give part of myself to another." Love says to the beloved: "This is my body" and in this gift creates the power to make new human beings together with the beloved. Love does not trivialize sex and use it just for "recreation" or "fun", but gives itself totally and exclusively and faithfully to the beloved—and thus love discovers an incredibly deep happiness that far transcends "fun". Total joy comes from total self-giving. Pure joy comes from pure self-giving.

7. "You shall not steal." Love respects the beloved's personal property and privacy, because love respects the very person of the beloved. Love does not take away; love gives.

8. "You shall not bear false witness against your neighbor." Love does not lie. Love does not deceive the beloved; love does not try to "fake out" and take advantage of the beloved. Love lives in truth as a fish lives in water. Love lives in the light, not in the darkness. Love cannot live a lie; love cannot live in lies. Love is like a plant: it needs light to live. As plants live by photosynthesis, love lives by truth. Love knows that it dies when the light and truth die; therefore, love insists on speaking and living in light and truth.

9. "You shall not covet your neighbor's wife." Love does not regret giving all of itself to one and does not covet (desire) another. Total love does not split itself into parts and send parts of itself out to others besides the beloved, even in the mind. Wishing you married another person is like wishing you worshipped another God.

10. "You shall not covet your neighbor's goods." Love is not greedy after things, especially things that belong to others. Just as love does not want to commit adultery (the ninth commandment), love does not want to steal. For love loves people, not things. It uses things, not people. It uses things for people, not people for things.

So you see, every one of God's Commandments is a commandment about love. The Commandments tell us what love does. The reason for this is that God, the Commander behind the Commandments, *is* love. And His fundamental moral rule is for us to be like Him: "You must be holy as the Lord your God is holy." To be holy is to be Godlike, and God is love; therefore, to be holy is to love.

10. *Why is Catholic morality unchanging and absolute and uni-versal? Why doesn't it change with the times, and with dif-ferent situations, and with different groups of people? Why is it so rigid?*

The rules of morality do not change with the times because its rules are not the rules of changing times but the rules of the unchanging essence of love itself.

We measure changing times by this unchanging rule. We cannot measure changing things unless we have unchanging standards. For instance, when we say a certain person is getting morally better or worse, we mean that he is coming closer to the standard or getting farther away from it. If the standard changed as well as the person, the standard could not mea-sure the person's progress toward it. If the finish line in a race moved as fast as the runners ran, there could be no measure of the runners' progress. You can't measure a squirming snake with another squirming snake; you need an unchanging, rigid yardstick.

The rules of true morality do not change with different sit-uations because they do not originate from changing situa-tions. They originate from the essential nature of love itself. We have to *apply* the rules differently to different situations, but the rules do not *come from* those changing situations. Rules are *for* particular situations; they cannot *come from* particular situations. The rules of math illustrate this. The rules of math do not come from the material world, where things move and change and grow, but we can apply these unchanging rules to different changing things in the world. A foot is one-third of a yard at all times and everywhere, whether we are measur-ing the growth of a human body or the length of a river and whether we are measuring it on Monday or on Tuesday.

Of course, the rules of math are much simpler than the rules of morality. A calculator can do math but not morality. But moral principles are like mathematical principles in another way: they are unchanging, for only unchanging standards can measure changing things. For instance, the moral principles of war (the principles that judge when it is morally wrong to fight a war and when it is morally right) are unchanging, but their application to changing kinds of war is changing. In a medieval age of all-volunteer armies and individual hand-to-hand combat, the application of the principle of justice to warfare was fairly simple and easy; but in an age of "total war" and the drafting of civilians and the existence of weapons of mass destruction that kill noncombatants, the application of the same principle of justice is more complex, more difficult, and more restrictive. Bombs need to be restricted more than swords.

Here is another example: In a precapitalist society where money is merely a symbol for gold or land, taking interest on money that is lent is called "usury" and is declared to be unjust because it takes advantage of wealth to the disadvantage of the poor. By usury the rich get richer and the poor get poorer, unfairly. But in a capitalist society where money can make more money if wisely used, taking interest on loans is not unjust. It can actually benefit the poor by giving them opportunities for economic upward mobility (chances to increase their wealth) that they did not have in precapitalist societies. So even though the basic principles of economic justice remain the same in all times, the principles have to be applied differently to changing times, for instance in capitalist societies versus precapitalist societies.

In both of the two cases we just mentioned, war and capitalism, the essential *principles* are unchanging, but the *appli-*

cations of those principles to changing social situations has to be changing. It is precisely *because* of fidelity to the principles that they have to be applied differently to different situations. The rules of morality are *universal* as well as unchanging. "Universal" means that the rules are for everyone, not just for some, because we all have human nature, and these are the rules for human nature. They are not just Christian morality, and not just Catholic morality, but human morality, human-nature morality. That's why we call it "natural law morality".

But Christian morality is the most complete human morality because Christ is the most complete man. Christ reveals to us not only who God is but also who man is, who we are. He is the fullest revelation of God *and* the fullest revelation of man, the only perfect God and the only perfect man.

Non-Christians can know much of this morality too—for instance, many Hindus and Buddhists deeply appreciate the moral value of nonviolence, and Confucians deeply appreciate the value of the family—but Christians can know morality more clearly and fully because they know Christ, who is not just one of many good human moral teachers but is God!

As Christian morality is the fullest human morality, Catholic morality is the fullest Christian morality, because the Catholic Church is the Church Christ authorized to teach in His name.

Non-Catholic Christians can know much of this morality too—for instance, many Protestants see the evil of divorce, abortion, sodomy, and euthanasia—but Catholics have a fuller morality. Part of that fullness is a sense of perspective, or emphasis on the more important goods and evils rather than on the less important ones. That is why Catholics have a stricter and less "liberal" morality than most other Christians in some areas, like divorce or abortion, that concern human love and life itself, and a less strict or more "liberal" morality than many other Christians in other areas, like gambling or drinking, that concern only material things. (Alcohol and gambling can be dangerous—addictive and destructive—but they are not *intrinsically* immoral.)

Catholic morality makes more distinctions than many churches do: for instance, it more clearly distinguishes the badness of sins and the goodness of sinners, and that is why it has *less* love and toleration for sexual sins (whether homosexual or heterosexual) and *more* love for sexual sinners (whether homosexual or heterosexual).

X

Why is sex so confusing?

1. Isn't the Church pretty unrealistic about sex?

On the contrary, the Church is the only institution in the world that is totally realistic about sex.

Realism means thinking about reality, thinking about what a thing really is. That is exactly what the Church does—and what our modern culture does *not* do.

The first and most important foundation for thinking about sexual morality is to understand what sex is. You cannot understand what anything *ought* to be unless you understand what it *is*. You cannot understand what "good *X*" and "bad *X*" is unless you understand what *X* is. And that applies to sex as well as to *X*.

2. But the Church's teaching is all about the ideal, not the real; about what sex is supposed to be, not what it is. If you want to start with reality, you must start with the brute facts. Sex is simply a fact of life, like hair and thirst and death.

Sex is *not* merely a "fact", like the color of your eyes. It is more like a *look*, a glance of the eyes. It has deep meaning and purpose. It means something, it points to something, like a sign or a word or a pointing finger. It doesn't just happen, like a belch, but it speaks, like a word.

The word it speaks is love. Sex *means* love. Sexual activity is one kind of love. We often call it "making love". It is a form of speech, of body language. And what it says is: "I love you with my body, with my sexuality; I love your sexual identity with my sexual identity; I love your whole identity, body and soul, with my whole identity, body and soul." Since it means that wholeness, it does not mean merely "My body wants your body for my body's pleasure." That is all that sex means for the animals, but it means something much more personal for human persons.

There are also many other kinds of love besides sexual love: for instance, instinctive liking, comfortable familiarity, friendship, charity, and admiration. We even say "I'd love a steak dinner" or "I loved that vacation" or "I love to listen to that music." In other words, we love things and we love persons, but obviously not in the same way. When we love persons as if they were things, when we use persons as mere means to the end of our own selfish pleasure, that is a profound misuse of love. For instance, slavery and prostitution both use people as means instead of loving and respecting them as ends.

3. All right, then, so sex is about love. But the Church says sex is about babies, that sex is for procreation.

Sex is about both. That's the Church's point.

What most clearly distinguishes sexual love from all other kinds of love is that by its very essence, by its nature, it is fertile. It leads to procreation as naturally as eating leads to nutrition or exercise leads to healthy muscles. That is simply a biological fact. It's called the "reproductive system". Sex makes babies. That is its nature. What it *does* is part of what it *is*. Its natural effect is part of its nature. If you leave sex alone, sex can lead to conception—unless you stop it by some form of contraception. That's why contraception is called "contra-ception": it works against conception. That presupposes that conception would happen by nature, without our doing anything more, unless we did something against sex, fought against it, fought against its natural effect.

Exercise, eating, and sex are also by nature pleasurable but in obviously different ways and degrees. Sexual pleasure is different from all other pleasures, just as the pleasure of eating is also different from all other pleasures, and so is even the pleasure of exercising. That is also a fact, a biological and psychological fact.

So just as the nature of eating includes both its unique effect (nutrition) and its unique pleasure (the satisfaction of hunger), and just as the nature of exercise includes both its unique effect (stronger muscles) and its unique pleasure, so the nature of sex includes both its unique effect (babies) and its unique pleasure. There are thousands of things that give us pleasure, but in general, the greater the effect, the greater the pleasure. No effect that we can ever produce is as great as new *people*, and no pleasure is as intense as sexual pleasure.

4. So how does that make sex sacred? Pig sex makes baby pigs too, but that doesn't make pig sex sacred.

Animal sex is not sacred because animals are not sacred. But human sex is sacred because humans are sacred. Sex is sacred because sex is not just *made by* humans but sex *makes* humans, makes more of those sacred things that we call human beings.

Let's look more closely at what sex makes, or procreates; let's look at those amazing things we call persons, or people. What is distinctive about persons? Why are they sacred? They alone, of all the things in this material universe, have infinite value, because they are not just God's creatures but God's *children*. Birds and flowers and rocks and stars and everything else in the created universe are creatures too and have value. ("Creature" means simply "created thing".) But we are not just God's creatures but God's children because God is not only our Creator but our Heavenly Father. We are not just created, but created in God's *image*.

5. *What does that mean, that we are created "in the image of God"?*

It means that, unlike all the other things in the universe, which are just material things, we are also spiritual, like God. We have spiritual souls as well as material bodies. And two of the powers of the spiritual soul are the mind and the will. We can think and we can choose. We can know and we can love.

And because we are spirit as well as matter, because we have souls as well as bodies, we are immortal. When the stars die, billions of years from now, every one of us will still be alive. Each individual lasts longer than any nation or empire on earth. That is why we have intrinsic value. You can't put a price on a person. Each person is worth more than the entire universe.

That is what sex makes: new persons, new children of God, new immortals.

Procreation is literally a miracle. Every time we naturally make a new human body by sexual intercourse, God supernaturally creates a new human soul. God creates whenever we procreate.

This is one of the two greatest miracles in the universe, for it is one of the two ways God Himself keeps entering the universe to perform a miracle, to do something only God can do. The other ongoing miracle is the Eucharist, where God transforms bread and wine into His own Body and Blood every time a priest says the words "This is My Body" and "This is My Blood" over the bread and wine in the Mass. This is why sex is holy, like the Eucharist. It is not "dirty"; it is holy.

Unholy people *feel* "dirty" in the presence of something holy, like a saint, or a miracle, or an angel, or the Blood of Christ. In the presence of great sinners, we feel like saints, but in the presence of great saints, we feel like sinners. In the presence of something very good and holy and clean, we feel unworthy and unholy and unclean.

6. *But sex doesn't always* make new people. *It doesn't have to. You can be sure it doesn't by using birth control. So sex isn't always holy.*

Yes it is, because it always is what it is. It never loses its nature, even when it is prevented from exercising its power. A person who is bound and gagged and tied to a chair is prevented from exercising his power of walking and talking, but he is still a person and still a walker and talker, unlike a chair. When sex is prevented from exercising its power of procreation by contraception, it is still sex, and still a holy thing. A priest who cannot offer the Mass is still a priest.

Contraceptive sex is artificial, not natural. The point here is not that everything artificial is wrong—of course not—but the point is simply that sex makes babies *by its very nature*. That is part of its significance, its meaning. Just as sex *means* love, just as it *means* "I want to give you my whole self, my body and my soul, my whole person, my whole personality, sexual and spiritual, material and mental, all of me, completely", it also *means* children, just as an eye *means* seeing or a sword *means* fighting or a word *means* communicating. It is not a meaning we add to sex, but a meaning that is in it by its own nature. Unless you do something to stop it, sex makes babies.

In fact, this second meaning flows from the first one: the "baby-meaning" flows from the "love-meaning". "I want to give you all of myself" *means* "I also want to give you my fertility" and "I want to give you my life, my children, my family, my future. I want to share my whole life with you." That is the "message" God put into human sexuality when He designed it.

These two meanings (love and babies) do not just happen to be both there together by accident, but they are *meant* to be there together (as two lovers sense that they were "meant to be together"). By its very nature, sex means both intimate, total, self-giving love *and* procreation (babies, family).

That is why cloning and creating test-tube babies are wrong. They are not just *un*natural but *anti*-natural. They are not wrong because they are artificial or technological but because they tear up God's design for sex. They say yes to one half of it and no to the other half. As contraception says no to babies and yes to sex, they say yes to babies and no to sex. What God joined together, they separate. It is like divorce. (Remember Jesus' words against divorce: "What therefore God has joined together, let no man put asunder" [Mt 19:6]). For it was not just one man and one woman, but also God, who made the marriage. It takes three to get married.

That is the same reason why rape and prostitution are evil.

They are unnatural, antinatural, against God's design for the nature of human sex. Homosexual sex, bestiality (sex with animals), and masturbation (sex with yourself) are wrong for the same reason. (They are not all equally bad, but they are all bad.) They are wrong because they are antinatural, and antinatural sex is so wrong only because natural sex is so right. They are so bad only because sex is so good. They pervert a very, very good thing. They deface a holy picture, an icon.

That is also why artificial contraception is antinatural and wrong. Sex that deliberately refuses all procreation refuses part of its own essential nature and thus violates the very nature of sex.

It's not just a question of how you *feel* about it, whether you feel comfortable with it or uncomfortable, whether you feel it's desirable or disgusting. Most people in our culture no longer feel that contraception is disgusting, as they used to. Most people in our culture still feel that bestiality is disgusting, but some don't. Some people feel that homosexual sex is disgusting, and some don't. But all three kinds of sex are wrong for the same reason. The reason is not how we feel, but what it really is. Morality is not based on subjective feelings but on objective reality. You can't tell whether something is good or evil just by looking at your feelings. You have to look at what it really is. The question of whether *X* is morally good or evil is a question about *X*, not a question about you! You can't find out what a thing really is by looking at how you feel about it, unless you are God. You can find out what anything is by looking at how *God* feels about it, because God designed it. But you didn't. (Unless you are God!)

7. *Does that mean that all birth control is wrong?*

No. Spacing and planning births is not unnatural and wrong. Natural family planning (NFP) does this by respecting the essential nature of sex and of the male and female human bodies and a woman's natural fertility cycle.

(By the way, nearly all couples who practice NFP are very happy and satisfied with it—and with each other. The divorce rate among NFP couples is 1–4 percent, in a society where it is nearly 50 percent. That tells you something!)

8. *You say sex is for babies. But it is also for pleasure. Sexual pleasure is as natural to sex as babies are. To suppress its natural pleasure is as unnatural as suppressing its natural fertility.*

This is true! Sex also obviously gives great pleasure. And that is no more an accident than babies are. That is part of God's design. When He invented sex, He put great joy into it from the beginning, because He thought so highly of it. He could have invented other ways for us to come into the world instead of sex, or He could have put less joy into this way that He invented for us, but He didn't. (That's why the Church respects it so much: because God does.)

He put such great joy into it because He put two other great things into it: intimate, total self-giving love, and the procreation of new persons, who will live forever. The Church puts a far higher value on sex than the world does. The better something is, the more respectful we are to it, the less we treat it like trash. We take great care with things of great value, like art masterpieces (but not casual sketches), or pets (but not animals out in the wild), or persons (but not mere things).

9. Why do the rules of sexual morality have to be so complex?

They are not complex at all. They are embarrassingly simple, uncomfortably simple. The moral law is not complex and difficult to think about; it is difficult to live. Ignorance is not the biggest enemy of morality; selfishness is. Most moral problems are solved not by cleverness but by honesty.

The essential Christian (and Jewish and Muslim) moral law about sex, from the beginning, has always been very simple: "You shall not commit adultery." "You shall not adulterate sex." Everyone knows what that means. It means don't cheat on your spouse. Don't have sex with others. You can't give your whole self to more than one other whole self.

The place for sex is marriage. The perfection of sex happens only in marriage, in a voluntary, committed, lifelong, faithful, heterosexual relationship of mutual, total, self-giving love. That is what marriage *is*: that is its essence, its nature, what God designed it to be. The connection between sexual love and marriage is part of the *essential nature* of both sex and marriage. Marriage is as natural to sex as air is to birds or the sea is to fish. So we must look at marriage in our next chapter.

10. Why does sexual morality have to be so negative? "Don't do this, don't do that."

There is only one reason for the "don't's", and it is a "do". There is only one reason for the negative, and that is a positive. There is only one reason why being unfaithful and giving your body sexually to many people is so wrong: because being sexually faithful and giving your whole body to one person is so right.

It's also wrong because of the Golden Rule, "Do unto others what you would have them do unto you." Everyone who commits adultery hides it from his spouse, because no one wants his spouse to do the same thing. It's a sin against justice. It's just not *fair*.

Worse than a sin against justice, it's a sin against love. Adultery (sex with others after marriage) is a sin against your spouse, and fornication (sex with others before marriage) is a sin against your future spouse.

And it's also a lie, a deliberate deception. For when you have sex with anyone, your body says, "Here is all of me for you", but when you're not married to that person, your mind does not say that. When you have sex with others, you lie. You lie with your body. When you have sex, you can't help saying with your body, "I give you my whole self, body and soul", because that is what the sex act says, what it means, by its nature. Yet with your intention, with your mind, you say something else. Your mind means the opposite of what your body means. If your mind *didn't* mean the opposite of what your body was saying in the sex act but meant the same thing, then you would be intending and proposing marriage to your lover! You are lying. You are dishonoring your own honor.

The fact that you are lying is obvious when you cover it up later. You don't want your spouse to know about it, not even your future spouse. That shows it was a lie, for it's always lies that you cover up, by telling more lies. You don't cover up truth.

XI

Why do we have families?

1. Why does the Church connect sex with families?

Because God did! Families are His invention. He designed us
to come into the world not from the stork but from sex, and
not all alone but into families; and He designed families to
come from sexual love. Like sex, the family is natural, part of
human nature. It is not a humanly invented, artificial thing,
like money or cars or baseball, but a God-invented, natural
thing, like speech or sleep or humor.

Marriage is the link between sex and families. Marriage creates families out of sex. Marriage makes sex personal, committed, and responsible. When two people marry, they promise
to give to each other their whole selves, body and soul, for
their whole lives, and they promise to give each other children, and to give themselves to their children, who will make
up an enormous part of their lives. They are not just *his* children or *her* children, or even his *and* hers, but *their* children,
forever.

2. Is the origin of marriage a choice, or is it love?

It is a choice to love. What makes a marriage is a love-choice,
not a love-feeling. Love-feelings ("falling in love") usually mo-
tivate the choice, but they don't *make* the choice. *You* do. What

transforms these feelings into a marriage is a deliberate, free choice of the will, which is expressed in the marriage ceremony in the words "I do."

Feelings are not free; choices are. We do not freely choose to feel, but we freely choose to act on our feelings or not to act on them. We can do the deeds of love with or without the wonderful feelings of love. Of course the feelings make loving much easier and more delightful. To choose to marry is to promise to do the deeds of love to this other person always. We hope we will also feel the feelings of love toward this other person always. But we cannot promise to feel a certain kind of love always because we cannot control our feelings as we can control our choices, our actions, and our words.

Therefore, the love we promise to give in marriage must be the kind of love we *can* choose and control. What kind of love is that? The gift of the whole of yourself to your spouse alone. It is called fidelity, or faithfulness. It means being with and remaining with the other in body and soul, "for better or for worse, for richer or for poorer, in sickness or in health, until death do us part". Being with the other in soul includes giving attention, care, and good will, putting the other first in your life.

The love that originally motivates the marriage and its promises is romance, but the love that fulfills the marriage and its promises is commitment. Romance makes you jump off the diving board, but commitment keeps you afloat and swimming in the pool.

3. That sounds all very nice, but that's not what marriage is to-day. It's a mess. The Church tells us what marriage is ideally, but the real is not the same as the ideal.

That is unfortunately often true. The Church tells us what God's design for marriage is, what marriage is supposed to be. By divine design, family is supposed to be the fulfillment of marriage and marriage the fulfillment of sex. And it often is. But what sex, love, marriage, and family have actually become much of the time in our fallen world, especially in our very confused American society, is far from what it is supposed to be. The real is not identical with the ideal in any society at any time after the Fall, for nothing in this world is perfect, especially human beings, their loves, their sexuality, their marriages, and their families. But these things are all more in crisis today than ever before.

But the Church also tells us what to do about the crisis, how to put marriage back together again. No matter how badly we have defaced, misused, and spoiled these three things—sex, marriage, and family—no matter how unhappy we have made these three happy divine inventions, they all remain very good things. They are three great gifts God gave us when He created us, in our original innocence, before the fall into sin. God designed them for our joy, and even in their fallen state they still give us great joy. In fact the greatest love and joy still always comes in families. (Think of Thanksgiving, or Christmas, or family vacations.)

Many families are in crisis today. The very institution of the family is in crisis. The percentage of American families that have been broken by divorce or desertion has increased from 5 percent to 50 percent in two generations. Modern society has made great moral progress in some areas—for instance, in our appreciation of human rights, equality, and compassion, especially to the poor and the handicapped. But there has been moral regress in other areas, especially marriage, the family, and sexuality. Previous generations were usually better than we are at the "hard" virtues (for instance, chastity, honesty, and courage) and worse than we are at the "soft" virtues (for instance, they tended to be more cruel and insensitive). This means we need to relearn the "hard" virtues and not keep using the "soft" ones as excuses for not practicing the "hard" ones.

4. Why did God invent families?

Every invention reflects the inventor. The Inventor of families is a Trinity, and the family reflects the Trinity, which is the nature of God, the nature of ultimate reality. Something like the family "goes all the way up". God is a kind of family —a nonbiological, spiritual family—a society of three divine Persons bound together by eternal, infinite love. The ultimate reason why God designed us to live in love, in families, and in societies is because He *is* love, He *is* a family, He *is* a society.

5. Why do families exist? What is the purpose of the family?

To be the place we are born into in this world. To be like landing strips for the airplanes from Heaven that we call children. God creates children and we procreate them. Whenever a man and a woman procreate a new human body, God creates a new human soul for it. A mother's womb is the center of a family, the place the family originates.

The family surrounding the mother and her womb is the place God designed to shape those most valuable things in the universe. Healthy bodies are shaped by "health care": food, exercise, and so forth. Healthy souls are shaped by the spiritual health care of love. Families are our schools of love, our first lesson in overcoming our natural egotism. Each of us is created as an individual, with our own will. With that will, we make millions of choices throughout our lives. This makes each life a drama, and the most important theme of the drama is the choice between good and evil, between unselfish love and selfish lovelessness, between centering our lives on ourselves and centering our lives on others, between treating ourselves as God, as the center of the world, and loving others as God loves them. The family is our great weapon in that battle.

Everywhere else, you are judged on your performance: you get promoted on the job only if you work well, and you get A's in school only if you get most of the questions right on a test. If you do not do a good job at work, you are fired, and if you get enough questions wrong in school, you get an F. But the family is the job that never fires you, and home is the school you never flunk out of. "Home is the place where, when you go there, they have to take you in."

This lesson of unselfish love that the family teaches is not only life's most important lesson to learn, but it is also life's most difficult lesson to learn. It's not intellectually difficult; it's morally difficult. It's very easy to learn to know it, but it's very hard to learn to do it. We know we should love unselfishly, but we don't do that very well. The meaning of life is to be a saint, but we find it hard to be saints. The basic problem in life, the basic problem in all the world, the basic cause of war and hate and violence and divorce and injustice and oppression and most of human suffering is selfishness; but we find it terribly easy to be selfish. We need a lot of practice and training in this fundamental lesson. The family is the first and most essential training ground.

6. How are private families connected to the larger public society?

The family is the bridge between the individual self and the rest of the world. All of social ethics is founded on the family, for all of society is an expansion of the family. Catholic ethics, like biblical Jewish ethics and Muslim ethics, has always been very strong both on the private family and on public social morality (for example, charity to the poor, social justice, the common good, and the individual's responsibility to work for and improve his community, school, country, and world). The present political tendency of the "right" or the "left" to emphasize one of these at the expense of the other is not natural. The Church is sympathetic to both the "conservative" emphasis on individual and family morality *and* the "liberal" emphasis on public, social morality. Neither can be a substitute for the other.

7. What is the relation between the family and the state?

The family is prior to the state. It is not the state that gives parents and children their rights, but God. Since the state did not give parents these rights, the state cannot take them away. That includes the parents' right to educate their children as they see fit. If the state offers free public education for parents to use, that's fine, but the state can be only the instrument of the parents, not vice versa.

The state is not the same thing as society. The state is necessary because we are fallen and sinful. (Think of how awful it would be if there were no police.) But society is a divine invention even before sin came into the world. There was no state in the Garden of Eden, but there was society. There will be no states in Heaven, but there will be society.

Society is like a larger, looser family; it is simply *other people*. The state is a specific, concrete institution. It is natural for man to live in states as well as in society, but the state is a legal authority over a limited geographical area, with the power to tax and to make war. The state is "political". The state is an *instrument* of society.

Society is much more important than the state. Many great men, like Jesus and Socrates, have been "apolitical" (unpolitical), but none have been unsocial.

8. How is all this connected with sex?

Families are created by marriages, and marriages are created by sexual love, so families are created by sexual love. And since the family is the foundation of society, society is created by sexual love. Sex and society are connected by nature.

That is why society, and the state that is the instrument of society, has a strong interest in sexual health and in sexual morality and sexual responsibility. Sexual irresponsibility must always result in social irresponsibility. If you lie to, betray, cheat on, and "rat on" your solemn, serious promise to your husband or wife, the one person closest to you, the one person to whom you promised to be true and to give your whole self and your whole life, then you will certainly lie, betray, cheat on, and "rat on" anyone else in society. If you harm your own children by breaking up your family, you will certainly harm other people and their children too. If you betray the people you loved the most, you will certainly betray those you love less.

9. *Is that why the Catholic Church does not recognize divorce?*

Yes.

Another reason is that the Church does not have the authority to change the teachings of Jesus. In all four Gospels, Jesus clearly forbids divorce.

The reason is clear: Jesus said, "What God has joined together, let no man put asunder" (pull apart) (Mt 19:6). This is a very simple truth but a radical one: *it is God who joins husband and wife together in marriage.*

Marriage is a sacrament, and it is God who is the primary agent who "works" in every sacrament; we are only His instruments. In the Eucharist, it is the priest who is His instrument; in marriage, it is the man and woman who marry who are His instruments, His priests, so to speak. It takes three to get married, not just two.

10. *How can there be divorced Catholics if the Catholic Church does not recognize divorce?*

There are three things that are often confused with a divorce: (a) a separation, (b) an annulment, and (c) a civil divorce.

a. A separation is not a divorce. It is two married people living apart instead of together. That is necessary sometimes because of physical danger, when one of the two is a threat to the other. A married Catholic does not have to keep living with a spouse who is constantly abusive. But when two married people no longer live together, that does not mean they can marry someone else or have sex with someone else. They are still married. Sex with someone else after you are married is adultery.

b. An annulment is not a divorce either. An annulment means that the original marriage was not really a sacramental marriage in the first place, because at least one of the parties did not enter it with full knowledge or full willingness to do one or more of the few basic, essential things that are necessary to have a real marriage: for instance, to have sex, to have children, or to be responsible for raising the children. If one of the spouses was mentally ill or addicted to drugs, he or she was not mentally free and competent to enter a Catholic, sacramental marriage. The Church grants an annulment only when, after careful investigation, she finds that one of these impediments to marriage was there from the beginning, when the two got married in the first place.

The Church is not infallible when it comes to practical decisions like this, though she *is* authoritative. (Parents are not *infallible* but they have *authority* over their children.) Mistakes can be made here. Often, annulments have been granted when they should not have been granted, just to make it easier on the people involved. The Church does not want to make life needlessly difficult for anybody. But the Church cannot betray her principles because they are not just *hers* but Christ's.

The Church cannot solve all our problems and fix all our mistakes. We are responsible for our own choices and their consequences. The choice to marry someone is the second most important choice in your whole life. The four most important choices in your life are the choice of a God to believe in, a spouse to love and marry, friends to trust and be loyal to, and a career to work at—in that order.

c. A Catholic can get a *civil* divorce, a divorce in the eyes of the state. That is not a real divorce. There is no such thing as a real divorce in the eyes of God. The kind of marriage that the state certifies is not a Catholic marriage, a sacramental marriage, a marriage that cannot be dissolved, the kind of marriage that Christ taught. It is only a human contract. God did not create that, only man did; so man can dissolve that.

Catholics who get a civil divorce, an annulment, or a separation are still Catholics. They are still in the Church, not out of it. The Church still ministers to them. They can still receive the sacraments.

And even when a Catholic gets a civil divorce and a civil remarriage to a second spouse without the Church's approval, the Church still offers her love, pastoral care, counseling, and most of her other ministries. But if one remarries without an annulment of the first marriage, the Church cannot offer the Eucharist, because even though the person may have good intentions, he or she is living in adultery and not repenting. Repenting does not mean merely feeling sorry; it means resolving to stop sinning. You can't intend to sin and repent of sin at the same time, whatever the sin may be.

The Church may seem cruel here, but she has to be honest. Honesty often seems cruel, but it is not. For honesty means telling the truth, even if it hurts, and in the long run, lies always hurt us more than the truth does. It is possible to avoid all lies, but it is not possible to avoid all hurts. We are fallen, sinful, imperfect creatures who sometimes make big mistakes, and we live in a fallen and imperfect world. In this world, life is often terribly unfair. We not only suffer, but we also often suffer unfairly. The Church, like her Lord Jesus, wants to be with us in our suffering, if we will let her, but she cannot tell lies about us or about our sufferings and our situations. Jesus never did that.

In the long run, the Church's absolute no to divorce is far kinder than allowing divorce, because divorce is one of the most painful things in life. The Church wants to spare us that pain. Like a doctor, she heals us of pain; but like a doctor, she sometimes has to do things that give us pain in order to spare us greater pain. The Church speaks in the name of Christ, and Christ was the kindest person who ever lived. But he was also the wisest, and therefore He knew what is best for us in the long run.

XII

Why are there virtues and vices?

Our format changes in this chapter. It is no longer the format of question-and-answer dialogue and argument. That is because the subject matter here—virtues and vices, a description of what a good person is and what a bad person is—is not as controversial as the other chapters. Nearly everyone knows what a morally good and morally bad person is. Most of the religions of the world teach a very similar morality. We all know, by our innate conscience, what good and evil mean, what we ought to do and what we ought not to do. This chapter simply summarizes or outlines what we all innately and instinctively know about good and evil. It clarifies what we already know; it brings it up from the level of unconscious knowledge to conscious knowledge.

1. The meaning of virtue and vice

Virtues are good habits; vices are bad habits.

Habits are patterns of behavior.

Character is the sum of your habits that direct your behavior. Behavior is something visible, external, in the world, while virtues and vices, habits, and character are all invisible, internal, inside your soul. But they are made visible by behavior. Your behavior shows your individual character to others; it makes the invisible visible.

Not all bad habits are *morally* bad habits. Some are just physical weaknesses (like stuttering) or habits of making mental mistakes (like dyslexia). Morally good and bad habits, like morally good and bad actions, are those that we are responsible for. We choose them. We make them. We bring them into being.

How do we make good and bad habits? By repetition. Every time you do a good deed or a bad deed, you make it easier to do it again the next time. You make the habit stronger. You form your character. You make yourself into one kind of a person or another kind of a person.

2. *The importance of virtues and vices*

Here's why moral virtues and vices are so crucially important: because they make you who you are.

A second reason is because they make you happy or miserable. In the long run, all virtues make you happy and all vices make you miserable. If you want your body to be happy, you have to make it healthy. If you want to make your soul happy, you also have to make it healthy. Virtues are the health of the soul; vices are the diseases of the soul.

(Your soul is everything in you that's not your body, everything that's not made of atoms and molecules, everything that's not material and visible. From your soul come your thoughts, your choices, your desires, your willing, and your feelings. Also in your soul are your *habits* of thinking, choosing, desiring, willing, and feeling. In each of these, your body plays a part too; it is your soul's instrument. For instance, the frontal lobe of your brain is the physical instrument your soul uses to think with. Your soul's power to think is what we mean by your "mind". Your mind is not your brain. Your mind is spiritual; your brain is physical. Your brain is a little like a computer. But unlike a computer, it is part of you, not outside you. Another example of the relation between your soul and your body is that your body's nerves and chemicals are the physical instruments your soul uses to feel with. Your soul's power to feel is called your "emotions". Your emotions are not part of your body, though they are strongly influenced by your body. A dead body, a body without a soul, has no feelings or emotions, just as it has no thoughts.)

A third reason virtues are important is that we can't help other people unless we are in shape ourselves. Just as a team can't win without each player doing his part well, so friends, families, and societies can't be happy, can't function well, and can't even survive for long unless the individuals that make them up are morally good individuals.

To see this point, think of two schools. The first one is big and rich. It has many large, luxurious buildings, lots of sports equipment, advanced technology, and well-written textbooks. All the students have their own state-of-the-art computers. But the people who make up this school, the students and the teachers and the administrators, are bad people. That one thing alone makes it a bad school. You would not want to go there. The second school is small and poor and has none of the luxuries the other school has, but all the people in it are very good people. They care about each other, and they care about education. That one thing alone makes it a good school. You would be happy there, and you would learn a lot more in the second school than in the first. Now think of the two schools as two societies. Which one is better? Obviously, the one that has the better people in it.

That's why the key to a good society, and even good politics and economics, is good moral character.

3. The relation between morality and religion

You have to be moral to be religious because morality is a part of every religion.

(It is not the only part. Every religion also has a theology, or teaching, or doctrine, or wisdom. And every religion also has a liturgy, or prayers and meditations and forms of worship. Morality, theology, and liturgy are three parts, or dimensions, to every religion in the world.)

So you do have to be moral to be religious, but you don't have to be religious to be moral. Nonreligious people can be moral people too.

However, religion makes it much *easier* to practice good morality. There are at least four reasons why.

a. Religion gives you a clearer, more complete *map* of good and evil, for one thing. It gives you God's mind, not just your own.

b. Religion gives you a stronger *motive* for being good: to please God, to become closer to God.

c. Religion gives you *higher ideals*, which are more interesting, more beautiful, and more inspiring than worldly ideals.

d. Finally, and most important of all, religion gives you a greater *power* to be good—divine grace—so you don't have to rely on just your own efforts.

4. The relation between moral virtue and salvation

You are not saved by virtue. Heaven is not a reward that you deserve for being good enough. How good would be "good enough"? None of us is good enough to deserve Heaven. Heaven is a gift of God's grace. No one deserves it. Yet anyone can attain it, because it is God's free gift. It is freely given and must be freely accepted. What God requires for salvation is only for us to accept His free gift of grace and live according to it. That is the "Gospel", or "good news". It is Christ who has saved us; we do not save ourselves.

You don't get to Heaven by being good; you become good by letting Heaven get to you. You don't buy your way into Heaven by deserving it; you become more heavenly by letting the Man from Heaven be the Lord of your life. Then your motive for being good is no longer fear of punishment but love of Him.

But although you are not saved by being virtuous enough, acceptance of salvation has three parts, and each of the three has something to do with moral virtue.

The first part is repentance. Repentance is an admission and a choice: the admission that we have sinned (disobeyed God's will) and the choice to turn away from sin, saying a sincere no to sin. *No* sin is so great that it can keep us out of Heaven if it is repented of. Christ's death on the Cross has atoned for all our sins, not just some. But *any* serious sin can keep us out of Heaven if it is not repented of.

(Repentance is not a feeling but a choice of will. Feelings come and go; choices last. Feelings come *to* us; choices come *from* us. We are not responsible for our feelings; we are responsible for our choices.)

The second part is faith, that is, the choice to accept Jesus as our Savior from sin. This means believing that He is the Savior and trusting Him. "Trust" does not mean emotional comfort; it means entrusting our souls to Him. That too is an act of free will.

The third part is the choice (again, of the will), the resolution, and the sincere attempt to live in charity, for that is the fulfillment of God's will. Charity is the internal choice to do the external works of love. We are not saved by doing enough good works, but good works are also essential to salvation, for "faith apart from works is dead" (Jas 2:26).

The connection between faith and works is like the connection between an invitation and a party. Faith means inviting Jesus into your heart and life, and if you do that, He will come and change your life. He will throw a moral party in your soul. Your life will be not just *your* life but *His* life as well as yours. Your charity will be His charity. Not just your *imitation* of His charity, but *His*. It will be from His Holy Spirit living in you, in small ways or large.

Our attempts to live in charity will not be perfect. We will sin. That is why Christ established the sacrament of Reconciliation (or Confession). It brings His forgiveness to us, as an umbilical cord brings oxygen to an unborn baby. He is really present there, just as He is in the Eucharist.

All three steps in salvation have something to do with morality. The moral law defines the evil we must repent of, the sin Christ saves us from, and the good we are saved *for*, the good we must sincerely attempt to live after being saved.

5. *The four cardinal virtues and their opposites*

We can distinguish three levels of morality: the natural moral virtues, the theological virtues, and the beatitudes. They are like the roots, the stem, and the flower of a plant.

The first of these three levels, the natural moral virtues, is found in every religion in the world. But they are not necessarily religious (though they are not antireligious either). It is natural morality, a morality based on human nature.

Four of the most important virtues on this level are called the "four cardinal virtues":

a. *justice* (fairness, rightness),
b. *wisdom* (practical wisdom, prudence),
c. *courage* (fortitude, bravery), and
d. *self-control* (moderation, temperance).

Their opposites are four of the most important vices:

a. *injustice* (unfairness, wrongness),
b. *folly* (foolishness, moral stupidity),
c. *cowardice*, and
d. *self-indulgence* (intemperance, addiction).

Justice rightly orders our relations with others, by rules such as the Golden Rule: "Do unto others as you would have them do unto you." (This is called the "Golden Rule" because it is as valuable as gold. It shows up all the evils that we do, for we never want evil done to us.)

Wisdom rightly orders our mind toward to the true good. It is like a road map.

Courage rightly orders our will to pursue the good and to oppose the evil, to "fight the good fight", the fight for goodness. For the morally good life *is* a fight, a spiritual war. Courage is the willingness to suffer and sacrifice, if necessary, in this war for the good. As wisdom is moral "mind power", courage is moral "will power".

Self-control is moral "desire power", the right ordering of our desires and emotions toward the good and away from the evil.

Mind, will, and human emotions are the three abilities of the soul that are distinctively human, that raise us above the animal. Animals have intelligence but not *rational* intelligence. They have something like willpower, but not free will, free choice. And they have emotions like fear and affection, but not *distinctly human* emotions that are filled with reason and free choice, like deliberate compassion or honor or *righteous* indignation.

These four cardinal virtues are not the *only* important natural moral virtues. For instance, we could add *honesty*, *responsibility*, *mercy* (or kindness), and *openness* (willingness to listen) as four more very necessary virtues on the natural level. Their opposites are *dishonesty*, *irresponsibility*, *cruelty*, and *arrogance*.

Nearly all moral thinkers, non-Christian as well as Christian, highlight the four cardinal virtues, for instance Plato and Aristotle, the two greatest pre-Christian ancient Greek philosophers.

6. The three theological virtues and their opposites

Faith, *hope*, and *charity* are called the "three theological virtues". They are called "theological virtues" because their object is God ("theos" is the Greek word for God). They unite our souls with God. They are like God-glue.

They are also called "theological virtues" because their *source* is God. They are gifts, or graces, from God. We can freely choose to accept or reject these gifts, but we do not create them by our own power. We do not push spiritual buttons somewhere inside our soul and make faith, hope, and charity appear by our own power. They appear only when we let God act in our souls.

Faith means two things: (a) *believing* all that God has said, or revealed, or taught us, and (b) *trusting* God personally, saying yes to Him with your heart, letting Him in. In the New Testament, faith is always connected with Baptism as the way God first enters our souls.

The New Testament sometimes uses "faith" in the first sense, the narrower sense of belief with the mind (1 Cor 13:13; Jas 2:14–26), and sometimes in the second sense, the broader sense of personal trust with the "heart" (Rom 1:17; 4:1–25; Gal 3:1–29). Belief alone does not save you; it is just a necessary first step. But it is necessary, because you have to believe someone before you entrust yourself to him.

Hope is faith directed to the future. It means belief and trust in God's promises, especially His promise to save us. (The name "Jesus" means "God saves.")

Charity is basic love, essential love, will-love, willing the good of the other. Charity is often confused with two other things: (a) private, subjective, personal *feeling* and (b) public, objective, visible deeds like giving things to the poor. These two things are very good, but charity is more than these two things.

Charity is more than a feeling because it is a free choice. Feelings are not freely chosen. You can't help how you happen to feel. You can't have the same feelings toward everybody. But you can and should have charity, or goodwill, toward everybody. Jesus didn't feel the same feelings toward each of His disciples any more than you feel the same feelings toward every individual in your family. But He loved them all with the same charity, or goodwill, and He died for all of them—and for all of us.

Jesus *commands* us to love our neighbors—all of them. What kind of love was He talking about? Not a feeling, for it is impossible to have a feeling just because someone commands you have it. "I command you to have nice, sweet, sympathetic feelings toward me"—that's just silly. And Jesus was never silly. The love He meant was charity.

It is very important to clear up the confusion between Christian charity and feelings, because that means we can have charity-love toward people even when we do not have love feelings toward them; we can *love* them even when we do not *like* them. We can will true good always to everyone, even though we cannot feel attraction always to everyone.

This is not a hard distinction to understand, because we already do this to ourselves: we don't always feel "in love with" ourselves, but we always will our own good, seek our own good. Jesus' "Golden Rule" is simply to "love your neighbor as yourself", that is, as you already do love yourself.

The second confusion we sometimes make is between love (charity) and the works of love, the deeds of love, charity as a deed. Charity is more objective than a feeling, but it is more subjective and personal than a deed. Charity is willing the good of the other. It *produces* external deeds (good works, the works of love). But other motives also can sometimes produce good deeds. The rich can give food or money to the poor just to show off, or to become famous, or to get a tax deduction. Saint Paul says, in First Corinthians 13:3, "If I give away all I have, and if I deliver my body to be burned [die as a martyr], but have not love, I gain nothing." Terrorist bombers give up their lives for their cause, but it is not out of charity; it is out of hatred.

The three theological virtues have three opposite vices, just as the four cardinal natural moral virtues have four opposite vices. (Vices are opposites of virtues. Virtues are good habits; vices are bad habits.)

Since "faith" means two things (intellectual faith, or belief, and personal faith, or trust), each kind of faith has an opposite vice. The opposite of belief (the first kind of faith) is unbelief.

The opposite of trust (the second kind of faith) is mistrust, or refusal to trust.

There are also two vices opposed to hope: despair and presumption. They are also opposites to each other. Despair is hopelessness, and presumption is arrogance. "I can never be saved" is despair; "I don't need to be saved" is presumption. Hope is the happy medium between these two extremes.

The two main vices opposed to charity are hate and indifference. Since charity is an act of will, so hate and indifference also are acts of will, deliberate choices. Hate is the active sin, or "sin of *com*mission," that is opposed to charity. When you hate someone, you positively wish him harm. You not only don't will him good, but you actively will him harm. Indifference is the passive sin, or sin of *o*mission, that is opposed to charity. The old word for indifference is "sloth" or "slothfulness". It means not just physical laziness but spiritual laziness, refusal to love the good even when it is known. You just don't care.

Both hatred and indifference chase love out of your heart, but indifference does it more dangerously because it does not *look* as bad as hate. Sometimes hate can be surprisingly close to love. It is not possible to love and to be indifferent to the same person at the same time, but it is possible both to love and to hate the same person at the same time.

7. *The eight beatitudes and the seven deadly sins*

In his famous Sermon on the Mount, in Matthew 5–7, Jesus taught eight "beatitudes", or blessings, that faith, hope, and charity bring—eight fruits of faith, hope, and charity; eight rewards for having the faith, hope, and charity that glue our souls to Him. These eight blessings are poverty of spirit, mourning, meekness, hunger, mercy, purity, peacemaking, and being persecuted.

Each of the eight is a surprise. They certainly don't sound like blessings. Each of the eight takes something we naturally fear and tells us it is a blessing—and gives us the reason why it is a blessing:

    a. Blessed are the poor in spirit, for theirs is the kingdom of heaven.

    b. Blessed are those who mourn, for they shall be comforted.

    c. Blessed are the meek, for they shall inherit the earth.

    d. Blessed are those who hunger and thirst for righteousness, for they shall be satisfied.

    e. Blessed are the merciful, for they shall obtain mercy.

    f. Blessed are the pure in heart, for they shall see God.

    g. Blessed are the peacemakers, for they shall be called sons of God.

    h. Blessed are those who are persecuted for righteousness' sake, for theirs is the kingdom of heaven.

Each of these eight blessings for virtue has an opposite vice, and seven of these vices are called the "seven deadly sins". They are seven of the deadliest, or most harmful, of all sins. These make you the most miserable, in the end, and the eight beatitudes make you the most joyful, in the end.

    a. "Poverty of spirit" means being willing, in your spirit, to be poor, whether you are in fact rich or poor. It means not loving money and the things money can buy, not being addicted to it, being detached from it.

    The opposite of poverty of spirit is the deadly sin of *greed*, or *avarice*, which is an addiction to possessions.

b. To "mourn" means to weep. You weep when you are sensitive to someone's pain. You have sympathy. You identify with him in his suffering. You suffer with him.

The opposite of this is selfish indifference, or hardheartedness, simply not caring about others' sufferings. It is not one of the traditionally named "seven deadly sins", but it is just as deadly as they are.

c. "Meekness" does not mean "weakness" but kindness, not being a bully but a gentle person, "turning the other cheek" and walking away instead of fighting back to defend yourself. (It is sometimes right and necessary to defend other people from bullies, to defend others' rights; and sometimes it is necessary to hurt bullies to stop them from hurting other people; but Jesus tells us to take a different attitude toward defending ourselves and our own rights: *not* to hurt the bully even if he deserves it.)

The opposite of meekness is wrath, or uncontrolled, unrighteous anger, hatred, the will-to-harm the other. This is the opposite of love, which is the will-to-good for the other. This is very different from righteous anger, or "righteous indignation", which is moral, and, though it involves being angry at people for their sins, wishes harm only to sins, not to sinners.

d. "Hunger and thirst for righteousness" means dissatisfaction with yourself and your own righteousness, your own virtues; knowing that you are not as good as God wants you to be and not being content with what you are—aspiring to higher things, having high and holy ideals, even heroic ideals.

We are all imperfect, we are all weak, we are all sinners. But some of us don't care and are content with that; we do not "hunger and thirst" to be righteous. Of course, "righteous" does not mean "*self*-righteous", or proud. It means being a saint. Being a saint means being like Jesus. Most of us are not saints because we don't really want to be, even though Christ wants us to be that, and calls us to be that, and offers Himself to us, through the sacraments, to make us gradually into that.

This indifference or laziness or not caring about righteousness is the sin of *sloth*, or spiritual laziness.

e. Giving mercy means going beyond justice. Most quarrels happen when both parties think they have been wronged, treated unjustly (unfairly). This happens between friends, family members, and nations. It is the cause of most wars. Each side demands justice, such as in the case of Israeli Jews and Palestinian Arabs in the Middle East. Usually, both sides are right; usually, there has been fault on both sides. Jesus says that the only solution that works to these problems is not justice but mercy, forgiveness. That's how God solved the problem of human sin: He did not give us justice (what we deserved, punishment) but mercy, forgiveness. He paid the just price for us, for our sins, on the Cross, to free us from justice, so that we would not have to pay that just price, that punishment. He went beyond justice to mercy. And now he asks us to do the same for each other, to "pay it forward" to others. For we can't pay it *back* to Him any more than we can pay our parents back for the gift of life they gave us; so we "pay it forward" to our children when we become parents. Jesus wants His unselfish mercy to flow into our lives like a river flowing into a lake and then out again into other rivers.

The opposite of giving mercy is *gluttony*, which means not just eating and drinking too much but wanting to possess everything, wanting to have it all, devoting your life to getting rather than giving. There are two kinds of people: the givers and the takers. Christ asks us to be givers, like Him. Gluttons are takers. They never have enough. They are grabbers.

Givers have a full life—and a full self. Grabbers have an empty life—and an empty self. That's why they grab: they are trying to stuff their own inner emptiness full of things to fill up the emptiness they feel within themselves. Gluttons (grabbers) are really empty, and givers are really full.

f. "Purity of heart" (that is, purity of love, desire, will, want, motive, or intention) means loving unselfishly, loving the other for the good of the other, not loving selfishly, for your own sake, for your own pleasure. Purity does not mean not loving, or not loving those of the opposite sex, or not feeling deep attraction to them (remember, virtues and vices are not feelings); it means loving them for *their* good. It means respect.

Lust is the deadly sin opposed to purity. It means desiring the other as a means to your own sexual pleasure. It is surprisingly easy to do that and to deceive ourselves into thinking we are loving the other person when in fact we are loving our own pleasure and loving the other only as a means to that end. The reason why this self-deception is so easy is because the pleasure is so intense. It can become an addiction that blinds us.

Lust is selfishness applied to sex. It means using the other person as a means rather than an end, loving the other for your sake rather than for his or her sake. It is a lack of respect.

g. "Peacemaking" means making peace between enemies, making love where there is hate. It is a rare and difficult art. You have to be like Christ to do it.

This is not peace with "the world, the flesh, and the devil" but peace with God, yourself, and your neighbor.

The world, the flesh, and the devil are the three sources of evil, sin, and suffering.

"The world" means not the planet earth (*that* is very good, for God created it) but the untrusting, unbelieving, and wicked societies we have created throughout human history.

"The flesh" means not our bodies but our weak, fallen, sinful, selfish human nature, soul and body together.

And "the devil" means the Devil—and other evil spirits. Yes, they are real, unless Jesus was a fool or a liar, for He not only warned us against them but actually cast them out.

Jesus came to make war on the world, the flesh, and the devil, not peace. He came to give us "the peace the world cannot give", the peace we could not give ourselves, namely peace with God, and therefore peace with ourselves, and therefore peace with our neighbors. These three things go together, and in that order, for as Thomas Merton says, "We are not at peace with others because we are not at peace with ourselves, and we are not at peace with ourselves because we are not at peace with God."

h. Enduring persecution and mistreatment means having patience and courage: patience with the persecutor who gives you pain, and courage to endure the pain and not fear it. Patience and courage go together: patience toward the persecutor, and courage toward the pain.

Jesus is talking about being persecuted only "for righteousness' sake" here, that is, persecuted for something good and not for something bad, persecuted when you are in the right and not when you are in the wrong.

(People will often hate you more for being right than for being wrong. They will forgive you for being wrong more easily than for being right where they are wrong. For it makes them feel good about themselves to be right when you are wrong, but it makes them feel bad about themselves to be wrong where you are right.)

Envy is the deadly sin that is in a way the opposite of this patience and courage—though the connection is not nearly as clear as the other six. When you envy someone, you want to have what he has, or to be where he is, or even to be who he is. You have no patience with what you have, or where you are, and no courage to face and endure the hard things that you suffer when others seem to be better off.

Envy is the stupidest sin in the world. It never caused a single person a single moment of joy, even false or fake joy, as most other sins do.

8. Virtue and society

There are three parts to morality: your relation to God, your relation to yourself, and your relation to others. The third part, your relation to others, has a private side (your friends and family) and a public side (your public communities: town, state, nation, and world). Social ethics orders and regulates this public side.

Social ethics, social responsibilities, good social action, is a necessary and important part of morality, because it is a necessary and important part of human life. As you grow morally, you grow out of merely selfish concern and extend your concern to other people: first your family, then your friends, then your larger communities of school and neighborhood, and then to larger and larger communities: your city, your nation, and finally your world, the whole human race. This is a necessary and important part of moral growth.

But it is not the *most* important part, for three reasons.

First, in this area of morality, the concrete applications are much more relative and changing than in the other areas. What social and political systems for public life will work best for people depend a lot on different times and places and cultures and personality types. Christianity has some basic political principles, but it does not have a single political program. Jesus did not say much about politics. He left us to figure most of that out for ourselves.

Second, society is not where morality originates. Society has a powerful role in encouraging us to act morally and in discouraging us from behaving immorally by laws that reward good behavior and punish bad behavior, but society did not invent morality. Morality begins in God and your relation with God. If your relation to God is good, your relation to yourself will be good, and if your relation to yourself is good, your relation to others will be good. Society cannot make us good, though it can make it easier or harder for us to be good.

Third, although working for the common good is more praiseworthy than working for the private good, nevertheless individuals are more important than societies. In fact, the main reason why social ethics is important is that societies are teachers of individuals. The students (the individuals who are taught good or evil by their societies) are far more important than their teachers (the societies who teach them). There are three reasons why individuals are more important than societies. The first is that societies are not created in the image of God, but individuals are. Second, societies are not ends in themselves, but means to the good of the individuals and families in them; but each individual is an end in himself, to be loved, not used. Third, societies do not last forever, but every individual lasts forever. Long after America is dead, long after the sun loses its light and heat, you will still exist.

9. Virtue and happiness

Here is life's first lesson: To be happy, you must be good. If you are good—really good, not falsely, self-righteously, proudly, priggishly good—then infallibly, you will be happy—really, truly, deep-down, long-range happy. And if you are bad, you will not be happy. Not really happy.

No one in the history of the world has ever found deep happiness without moral virtue. And all who have practiced moral virtue have discovered that they are as a matter of fact truly and deeply happy. The better they are, the happier they are. The happiest people in the world are the saints.

10. Proof of the connection between virtue and happiness

That proof is not a matter of faith but a matter of experience. You can test it in your own life. Try it. You'll like it.

XIII

Why pray?

1. Praying doesn't turn me on. Why do it?

That's like saying "Why go to Church? It doesn't turn me on."
Going to Church and praying are both like eating. Your body
will die if you do not eat. That is an objective fact. And that
fact is the objective, realistic, and practical reason for eating.

You also eat for a second reason, a subjective reason: because
it gives you pleasure, because food tastes good. But the main
reason is the objective reason: you eat to live. Even if it doesn't
taste good, you have to eat or you will die.

The same is true of prayer, both personal, private prayer and
also the public prayer of the Church, the Mass, including the
reception of the Eucharist. These two forms of prayer do to
your soul what eating and drinking do to your body: they keep
your soul alive. Without them, your soul will dry up and die.

It's like friendship, romance, or marriage. These are relationships between two persons, and these relationships will die
if you don't seek out the presence of the other person. Relationships will die without communication. And your relationship with God will die if you don't spend time together and
communicate, just as a friendship, a romance, or a marriage
will die. And that is what prayer is: communication with God.

The ultimate reason to pray is *because God is real*. Prayer isn't
playing some little trick with your mind; it's putting yourself
into the presence of God. Prayer is not like exercise. You can

exercise alone. Prayer is essentially choosing to be with God, just as friendship, romance, and marriage are choosing to be with another person. Prayer is the "practice of the presence of God" (to quote the title of a great little book on prayer by a simple and holy man named Brother Lawrence). That's true of all prayer, whether the prayer is in words or without words and whether the prayer is public or private, individual or communal.

2. How do we do it? How do we pray?

In the same way that we communicate with our friends: with words! (And also without words.) So we pray in words. (And also without words.) The words can be our own words, or they can be the words of the Church or of the saints, the best words of the best poets of prayer, words that we make our own by using them. There is no reason not to use *all* forms of prayer:

    a. without words;
    b. in our own words, privately;
    c. in our own words with someone else;
    d. in the Church's words, privately; and
    e. in the Church's words, publicly and communally, especially at Mass.

Others' words, the words of the great saints, are like crutches or walkers. They help us to move. We should not be too proud to use them. But the most important thing is not the words. The most important thing is our love, which is shown by our presence, our desire and our willingness to be there with our friend. The proof you really *care* is that you're really *there*.

Love uses words, but love also goes beyond words. In fact, the deeper and more intimate the relationship is, the more important those times of silence are—those times when you don't need to say anything, because just being there with the one you love is enough. It is the same with prayer. It is your wanting to be with God that counts most, not the words.

A holy priest in France (the Curé of Ars) noticed a peasant who would often sit alone in church for hours, praying silently to Christ in the Eucharist. The Curé sensed that the peasant was a great pray-er, so he asked him what he did when he prayed. He answered, "I just look at Him, and He just looks at me." That is the heart of silent prayer: the look of lovers at each other.

3. What difference does prayer make?

When you pray, you give God a chance really to do things to you. He will change you in ways that are deep and radical and lasting. Even your earthly friends and loved ones do that to you when you let them.

Prayer is like a live wire: real power moves along it. Houses sometimes have warning signs: "Beware of the dog." Churches should have warning signs: "Beware of the God!" "Beware of prayer." "Look out; it's alive!" For God is even more alive than a dog, because God is more real than a dog. (After all, "dog" is only "God" spelled backwards.)

What things will God do to you? They are not usually sudden and spectacular but slow and deep and hidden—like the way your human loved ones change you when you love them.

One of the things He will do to you in prayer is this: He will make you honest with yourself. For in prayer, you place yourself in the presence of God, who knows everything (He is omniscient). You can hide from others and even from yourself —in fact, we are terribly clever at doing that sometimes!—

but you can never hide from God. God knows every single thing that is in you and everything about you, and He knows it completely and perfectly, because He created and designed you, as a writer creates his characters. Prayer brings you into God's light, the light of truth. Prayer makes you real, because God is real.

4. What is the purpose of prayer?

There are *four* purposes of prayer. They are (a) adoration, (b) confession, (c) thanksgiving, and (d) supplication, or petition (asking for things, saying "please"). You can remember them by the acronym ACTS.

Adoration is what we described above: just being there and loving Him, adoring Him, praising Him, worshipping Him, enjoying Him, admiring Him, looking at Him.

Confession means honestly confessing our sins, faults, and failures.

Thanksgiving means thanking Him for His blessings, counting your gifts and remembering who the Giver is.

Supplication, or petition, means asking for things, both for yourself and for others. Asking for others is called "intercession."

When people think of prayer, the first thing they think of is asking God for things. This is not the only purpose of prayer, but it is one of them, and it is good, for God Himself has told us to ask Him for things (Mt 7:7–11; Lk 18:1–8).

Beginning with adoration, confession, and thanksgiving rather than supplication is wise. It takes your mind off your own desires and puts you in the presence of the God you're praying to. He is more important than the things He gives. He's God, not Santa Claus.

5. *What is the purpose of supplication, or petition?*

First of all, to do what God asks. God commands us to ask for things. (See the two Gospel passages quoted above.)

Second, to be realistic. Asking God for good things is an exercise in realism, because God is in reality the giver of all good things, and we in reality need and want these things. Prayer is an exercise in humility, which is a very important form of realism. It is a confession of our neediness and our dependence on God. Think of the French sailor's simple prayer: "O God, Your sea is so big, and my boat is so small."

Third, to really change things. Prayer changes things.

What things? We cannot change God's mind, because God is perfect and unchangeable. But prayer changes everything else, everything that is changeable.

Prayer first of all changes our own mind and our attitude. We pray not to conform God's mind and will to ours (how foolish that would be!) but to conform ours to His. When we pray, we let God change *us*.

Prayer changes not only us, but it also changes the world. It is far more powerful than we think. In fact, if God let us see how powerful our prayers were, if He let us see all the differences our prayers made in the lives of all the people we prayed for, and in the lives *they* touched and in all the lives *those* people touched—if God let us see all the ripples made by the little pebbles of our prayers as we threw them into the water of time—we would probably be so stunned that we would not be able to get up off our knees for the rest of our lives.

6. *Why did God tell us to pray? He knows what we need. If He loves us, why doesn't He just give us the things that He knows we need? Why does He sometimes wait until we pray for them before He gives them to us?*

For two reasons. First, because He sees that we need prayer even more than we need the things we pray for.

Sometimes God does not give us the things we ask for right away, and sometimes He does not give them at all. This does not mean He does not hear us or care about us but that He is wiser than we are, and He sees that it is often better for us to wait, or not to get the thing we ask for. We do not see this. If we did, we would be as wise as God! So petition is an exercise in trust.

Second, God commanded us to pray so that we could make a difference, so that we could be real causes of getting good things. Prayer is like work: God could have given us food and shelter miraculously, without our having to work, but He saw that we needed to work even more than we needed the things we work for. Work gives us dignity and power: we really make a difference; we really change things. Well, God instituted prayer for the same reason as He instituted work: to give us the dignity of being real causes of change.

7. *If we don't always get what we pray for, does that mean that some prayers are not answered?*

No. God answers all prayers. Sometimes His answer is yes, and sometimes His answer is no, but He always gives us an answer. And the answer always comes from the same source, the same reason: His love and His wisdom. Since His love is wiser than ours, He sees when it would be better for us *not* to get the thing we ask for, or not to get it until a long time has passed. We don't usually see that. (We're not God! I hope that's not news to you.)

God is our Father in Heaven. If your father gave you all the candy you wanted when you were two years old, you would get sick. In fact, if he gave you everything you asked for when you were a child, you probably would not have lived very long. ("I wanna drive the car! I wanna fly off the roof like Superman!")

We don't understand why getting the things we want isn't good for us. Of course we don't. We are like little children compared to God. If we understood why God doesn't give us all the good things we ask for, we would be as wise as God.

8. *Is it all right to pray for material things? Is it all right to pray in emergencies? Isn't prayer supposed to be just for "spiritual" things?*

God takes material things very seriously. Jesus healed bodies as well as souls. He came in a human body to die a bodily death and rise bodily from the grave. His saving words to us were not "This is My mind" but "This is My Body." God created the material world, and our bodies, and our needs for material things. He told us to ask Him for the material things we need: "Give us this day our daily bread." He communicates His love to us each day through physical things: sunlight, food, water, health, smiles, hugs, and kisses.

There is a danger in the term "spirituality". It could mean an unhealthy separation between matter and spirit; between body and soul; between the concrete, visible things in the world and the abstract, invisible things in the soul. "Spirituality" could mean a scorn of the body and matter and the world, and that is not Christian. God "so loved the world that He gave His only Son" to die for the world (Jn 3:16).

The Christian religion is not "spiritualistic" any more than it is materialistic. God made us both matter and spirit, at once and together; and the religion God revealed to us fits our double nature, for it is both spiritual and material at once.

Since God took material things very seriously, we should too. We should pray about them. God is interested in every single thing in our lives, even our hangnails and hamburgers.

Should we pray in emergencies? Of course. But not only in emergencies. If we have a habit of prayer, we will meet the emergency with trust, courage, peace, and hope, because those are the things God pours into us, gradually and invisibly, when we pray. If we pray only in emergencies, we will not experience that. God may still answer our "emergency prayer", but He does not want to be just an "emergency God". He wants to be the God of our whole life, because He loves us completely and is intensely interested in everything in our lives. Jesus did not call God "our fireman" or "our policeman" but "our Father".

9. *How often should we pray?*

Saint Paul answers that question: "Pray constantly" (1 Thess 5:17). There is a kind of prayer that we can pray all the time, without words: "practicing the presence of God", just choosing to be in His presence. We can do that all the time, without interrupting anything else; we can do that *while* we are doing anything else at all (except sinning). For we *are* in His presence all the time, so we can *choose* to be in His presence all the time, since that means only choosing to be what we are.

Of course we don't consciously think of God all the time. But when He reminds us that He's there, we can easily utter a short, sincere "Thank you!" or "I love you!" or "I trust you!" every time we remember Him, that is, every time He reminds us. These mini-prayers are as precious to Him as a baby's smile is to his parents, because God loves us even more than parents love babies.

We should also set aside a set time every single day for prayer. The two best times are the beginning of the day—as soon as we are wide awake, before we do anything else—and at the end of the day, before we go to sleep. Morning prayer is good because then we can offer up to God our whole day that is coming. Evening prayer is good because then we can offer up to God our whole day that is finished, as well as our night's sleep that is beginning.

How long should we pray? At least as long as it takes to relax in His presence, to "be still and know that I am God" (Ps 46:10), to get free from our hectic slavery to the clock that we call our daily schedule.

Can you give God five minutes each morning and five minutes each evening? No one in the world can honestly say that he *can't* give God ten minutes a day, only that he *won't*. "But I just can't find time to pray. I'm doing so many other things every minute." It may be true that you can't *find* time to pray, but it's not true that you can't *make* time to pray or *take* time to pray. How much time do you spend watching the television or playing video games? Let's get our priorities straight!

Petition and intercession (petition for others) especially fits morning prayer, and thanksgiving especially fits evening prayer, for we can ask God to bless our day in the morning and we can thank Him for His blessings in the evening. And not just in a vague and general way ("Thank you for all Your blessings") but specifically, for example, "Thank you for Kevin's kindness, and Sarah's smile, and Dad's time that he took with me, and Mom's advice, and that juicy steak, and the cool rain, and that beautiful red bird—how did You invent those?—and Father McMullin celebrating Mass, and even Sam's sweet but stupid joke." In the words of an old hymn, "Count your blessings, name them one by one, and it will surprise you what the Lord has done."

Nothing is better for your body, soul, and spirit than thanksgiving. Nothing makes you healthy, happy, and holy more quickly and easily than gratitude.

10. *What should we say when we pray?*

The very best prayer is the one Jesus Himself gave us. We call it the "Lord's Prayer" because the Lord Himself gave it to us. We should pray it often, not quickly and mechanically and automatically, but slowly, thinking about every word and meaning it with our whole heart. And we should decorate or festoon or ornament each sentence in it with our own additions, in our own words, as we would decorate a Christmas tree.

We should also get to know a favorite saint to ask him or her to pray for us. Read about that saint's life. There are saints for every personality type and every occupation. Pick one you can admire and identify with. Perhaps it will be the saint you were named after. Make this particular saint your special friend in Heaven. This is not just a nice little game. The saint really is in Heaven and really is interested in your life and will really help you and will pray to God for you. (That's what "intercession" is.) Doing this will make a real difference to your life, even though you will usually not see this in a clear, visible way, like a miracle.

XIV

Why aren't we happy?

1. The title of this chapter sounds different from all the others. It doesn't sound like it's about religion. Why is it here in a book about the Catholic religion?

Because this question *is* about religion. This question is about the human quest that religion answers: the quest for happiness.

This quest takes place not in jungles or caves or canyons but in a much deeper and more mysterious place: the human heart.

Think of the heart that goes on this quest as a hunter. ("The heart is a lonely hunter", to quote an old book title.) The beast it is hunting is called happiness.

Or think of this quest as a locked door, a door everyone wants to open but cannot. The lock in a door is a strangely shaped thing. So is the key that opens it. And both the human heart (the lock) and the Christian religion (the key) are strangely shaped things, surprising things, mysterious things. But *the key fits the lock*. They match. This chapter is about the lock, and the rest of the book is about the key. The lock is the human heart, especially its deepest quest for happiness. The key is religion, true religion, a true relationship with the true God. That key alone unlocks that door.

Everyone seeks happiness. And everyone seeks it as a goal, as an end in itself. Nobody seeks happiness as a means to any further end. We don't want to be happy because we think it will lead to other things, but we want other things because we think they will lead to happiness.

For instance, no one says, "What good is happiness? It can't buy money." But some people say, "What good is money? It can't buy happiness." Others think money *can* buy happiness.

The reason one person enlists in the army and another dodges the draft is the same reason: they are both seeking happiness, but in opposite places. The reason one person marries and another does not marry is the same. Even those who commit suicide do so only because they want happiness, and they despair of finding it in life.

We don't seek something we have already found. So if we are still seeking happiness, that means we haven't found it yet —not enough of it, at least, not perfect happiness, not yet. We can all honestly sing with Mick Jagger "I can't get no satisfaction" much of the time. And also his other profound line, "You can't always get what you want." We all want happiness, all the time, but we don't all get it, and even when we do, we don't get it all the time.

And yet we can't stop seeking it. The beast we hunt has never been caged and tamed. Yet we can't stop hunting it. That's just how we're made; that's just our human nature. We are hunters.

We all experience some mixture of happiness and unhappiness. No one is totally happy or totally unhappy. But some have more happiness, deeper and truer happiness, more lasting happiness, than others do.

Why? What makes the difference? Why are some people so very unsuccessful in this quest?

Obviously, because they do not use the right means, the right road, the right key to open this door.

So the first thing to do is to find the right road. And the second thing is to walk down that road. First, you get out the road map, then you follow it. But you can't follow it if you don't know it. A book like this can't teach you to follow it, but a book can teach you to know it.

So what *is* the road to happiness? What brings us to happiness, or happiness to us? Different people give different answers to that question. That's why it is so important to find out which answers are true and which answers are false: because we can make mistakes about this, and this is one of the most important questions we can ask, because happiness is the thing we all seek all the time.

2. *Happiness is just a feeling, and different people feel differently about different things, so different things make different people happy. "Different strokes for different folks." For some people, happiness is a warm puppy; for other people, it is extreme sports. How can there be one road map for everybody?*

There is one mistake in that argument: happiness is not just a feeling.

Here are five things that show that happiness is not just a feeling.

a. Feelings come and go, but happiness—deep happiness—stays. Feelings are fleeting. They are like waves on the surface of the sea; happiness is like the solid calm at the bottom. Waves are great to surf on but impossible to build on or live on.

b. Happiness is the deepest thing in us. We long for it with all our heart, as our end or goal, not just as a means. But feelings are not the very deepest thing in us. Feelings usually *accompany* happiness, like friends. Happiness-feelings are the friends of happiness, but not happiness itself.

We modern Americans are much more worried about our feelings than any other culture in history ever was. It might be a really liberating experience just to forget our feelings for a while, not because they are bad or worthless or unimportant but because there are so many things that are even more important.

c. Feelings are not in our control; they just happen. You can't just command yourself to feel differently. But happiness does not just happen by luck or chance. ("Hap" is the old English word for "luck" or "chance".) We can be in control of our happiness. You are probably shocked at that statement. But I will explain it in the next paragraph.

d. The reason why we can be in control of our happiness is that the most important cause of happiness is goodness. Good people are happy; evil people are not. And we are in control of our goodness. We are *responsible* for being a good person; we are free to choose between being good or evil. Therefore, we are in control of the most important part of our happiness or unhappiness, because we are in control of its most important cause, our own goodness or evil.

Of course there are other causes of our happiness or unhappiness that we are not in control of: the things that happen to us against our will. Terrible tragedies often strike good people. But even these will harm us much less if we are good and will harm us much more if we are bad. A large, clean, deep lake can take a lot of garbage without becoming polluted, but a small, dirty, shallow lake cannot.

e. Some things do in fact make us truly happy, and some do not. So we can be wrong about it, we can make mistakes about it, we can think something can make us happy when it can't. So we are disappointed. (If that were not so, we would simply be happy all the time!)

But whatever we can be wrong about is objectively real, not just our own subjective feelings. Being wrong means that our subjective ideas fail to match the objective reality.

Therefore, happiness is not just our own subjective feelings.

So it's crucial to find out what road really does lead to true happiness and what roads do not. So we will explore seven of the most common roads, seven of the most common answers to the question "What is the road to happiness?" The possible answers are: wealth, fame, respect, health, pleasure, power, and religion.

(When we say "religion" we mean *real* religion. Real religion is a real relationship with the real God, the God who is real. The real God is the God of Jesus Christ, and a real relationship is a relationship of trust and love.)

3. Why can't money make you happy?

There are three reasons for thinking it can:

a. It's the first thing everybody thinks of when they think of happiness. When you see somebody with a big smile on his face, the first thing you say is: "What happened to you? Did you just win the lottery?"

b. Money can buy a lot. In fact, it can buy everything money can buy.

c. We know from experience that we're happier after we get the things we want than when we didn't have them. That's why we buy them! It's a no-brainer.

But:

a. Just because people *think* of money when they think of happiness, that doesn't mean money really does buy happiness.

People also say, "What good is money? It can't buy happiness." People contradict themselves. People are not infallible. People are not God.

b. Money can buy everything money can buy, but money can't buy any of the things that money can't buy. It can buy material things, but it can't buy spiritual things: peace, joy, love, beauty, friendship, trust, loyalty, honor, faith. And happiness! Above all, money can't buy people. It can buy only people who sell themselves for money, like prostitutes, or who sell other people for money, like slave traders, or Judas Iscariot.

c. Money can indeed relieve many cares. Poverty is no fun. But that's not enough. Anesthetics relieve pain too, but they're not enough to cure the underlying disease. Money can take care of many of the surface pains in our life but not the deeper pain. The rich commit suicide much more frequently than the poor.

The reason money can't make us happy is that it is only a means, but happiness is an end. Money is a "means of exchange". A "means of exchange" is a means, not an end. Happiness is an end, not a means. Therefore, happiness is not the same as money.

4. Why can't fame and glory make you happy? Everyone wants them. They make you more Godlike.

No, they don't. *Love* makes you more Godlike. God's Word does not say, "God is fame." It says, "God is love" (1 Jn 4:8).

Fame is fleeting. It's a fashion, a fad.

And fame depends on others, not on you. Do you want your happiness to depend on how many other people know you?

Fame is often fake, often false. A clever advertiser can take a lamp post and make it famous. You can get famous just by doing something so stupid that you get into a tabloid like the *National Enquirer.* Or you can get famous by murdering someone and getting executed for it.

People who are famous are usually less happy, not more happy, than other people. They wish they could walk down the street without people recognizing them and bothering them. They have no privacy. They often feel as if they have no life except in other people's eyes.

5. *Why can't power make you happy? Now that's Godlike. "Almighty God—" power is almost His middle name. And what's worse than losing power, losing control? It's like being a slave.*

Like money, power is felt more when we lose it than when we have it. No one enjoys being a slave or losing control. But just having power isn't enough to bring happiness. Like money, power is better at taking away unhappiness than bringing happiness. (Power and money can be exchanged for each other— power can get you money, and money can get you power—so they share many of the same limitations.)

Like fame, power simply does not make people happy. We can observe that. For like rich people and famous people, powerful people do self-destructive things more often than ordinary people do.

Power alone is not Godlike, because God is not power alone; God is the power *of goodness.* Power is open to good *or evil* uses. Power cannot be our true good because it can sometimes be evil as well as good. How could good ever be evil?

Though power is not evil in itself, it can readily be used for evil. In fact, it tempts people to do evil. "All power tends to corrupt, and absolute power corrupts absolutely." Dictators, who have the most power, are notoriously evil.

(The Pope is not a dictator; he is the "servant of the servants of God"—the God who became our servant, washed His disciples' feet, and died for us. Dictators are like vampires: they take your life, your blood. The God whom the Pope serves is the opposite: He *gave* us His life, His Blood.)

Power is like money: it's a means to an end, since it can be used for either good or evil ends. But happiness is our end. To identify happiness with power is to confuse the end with the means.

6. *Happiness is being loved, then: being respected, being accepted, being honored.*

No, because that too, like fame, comes from somebody else. It's in *his* mind that you are honored. How can *your* own personal happiness be in *someone else's* mind?

And you want to *deserve* the honor, don't you? You want to be honored for what you really are. So it's not the honor that makes you happy, but the thing you are honored for. Honor is like a grade in a course: it's only a sign of something else. A high grade is a sign that you have a good knowledge of the course. It's the knowledge that you need, not just the sign of it. A sign on a medicine bottle tells you only what's inside. It's not the label that heals you; it's the medicine.

7. *Why can't a strong, healthy, beautiful body make you happy? That's not in somebody else's mind—that's in you.*

We're getting closer. At least your body is you and not something external to you, like honor or fame or wealth. But health is still only in your body, not in your soul. If you have a healthy body, but you don't know it and feel it and enjoy it, it doesn't make you happy. The *knowledge* that you are healthy in your body, and the feeling of enjoying your bodily health, both exist in your *soul*, in your mind and feelings, not in the atoms of your body.

Your body is not your personality, not your very self. That's why you call it "your" body: you possess it. There's a "you" that possesses it. And that "you" is where happiness is. We have to climb further inside.

Here is a clue from the animal kingdom that shows that happiness is not first of all in your body. Humans can be much happier (and also much unhappier) than animals. Animals can only be contented (or discontented). But although we are greater than any animal in our capacity for happiness, some animal is always greater than we are in every bodily perfection. For instance, elephants are bigger, turtles live longer, lions are stronger, eagles are faster, hawks have better eyesight, dogs have better smell, sharks can eat everything, and cockroaches are almost indestructible.

And your body is not going to stay strong and healthy and beautiful forever. It's going to become weak and sick and ugly. It's going to become a corpse. Is your happiness going to be buried in a cemetery?

8. *Why can't enjoyment and pleasure make you happy? That's in you, not in other people, and it's in the soul, not just the body, and we seek it as an end, not just as a means. So it's like happiness in all three of those ways.*

Yes, and now we're getting closer, more inside. Pleasure is felt in the soul. But it comes through the body. It's dependent on material things, things in the outside world. It depends on good luck, on things we can't control.

Bodily pleasures go the way of the body: into the grave. Even before that, pleasures are fleeting. Pleasures don't last. But happiness does.

Also, some pleasures are false. We regret them; we are sorry afterwards. That is never true of happiness.

And pleasure can get boring. True happiness does not.

Pleasure is incomplete. When we have pleasure, we still don't necessarily have other good things, like wisdom and courage and peace and love. But perfect happiness is complete. So perfect happiness is not just pleasure.

So even though pleasure is close to happiness, or perhaps even an ingredient in it, it's not the whole of it. When we are happy, we are also pleased, but being pleased (pleasure) is not quite identical with happiness. Pleasure is to happiness what the scent of a flower is to the flower. It's an effect of happiness, a consequence of happiness. When you have real happiness, you feel pleased. The feeling comes from the reality. But we have not yet found the reality.

9. Then maybe nothing in the world can make us happy. Maybe the whole world can't make us wholly happy.

That is true! And that is real progress toward finding an answer. For it tells us where the answer has to be by telling us where it isn't. If this world is not enough to make us totally happy, then only something outside the world can do that. And that doesn't mean just something outside this planet but something outside this universe. And there is only one thing outside this universe: the Creator of the universe, God.

"You have made us for Yourself, and [therefore] our hearts are restless till they rest in You", Saint Augustine said to God. This restlessness is a very good thing. It moves us along, moves us to our true home. Our unhappiness is a prod down the road to God. If we were content, we would be like horses that lie down along the side of the road and chew the grass instead of moving on, moving home.

10. *What* can *make me happy?*

Only God, only the real presence inside you of the real God, known or unknown. Only the One who made you for Himself can satisfy your restless heart. Nothing else is big enough. Trying to fill that deepest longing inside you with the things of this world is like trying to fill the Grand Canyon with marbles.

Nothing *less* than yourself fulfills yourself. And the whole world is less than yourself. That's why Jesus said, "For what shall it profit a man, if he gain the whole world, and suffer the loss of his soul?" (Mk 8:36).

There is only one thing that is greater than the human self: God. Nothing less can make us fully happy. And whenever we *are* happy, it is only because God is giving a little of Himself to us through the things He created, especially other people and their love.

We are made that way. He created us to be restless until we rest in Him. He designed us that way, and we cannot change that design.

But how can we get Him? We can get things less than ourselves, but how do we "get" God?

The bad news is that we can't get God. We can only get, and control, and have power over, things less than ourselves.

But now comes the good news. He has done the work. He has "gotten" us. We can't climb up to Heaven to "get" Him, but He came down to earth to "get" us.

So what do we have to do now to get plugged into God and happiness?

Here's the best part of the good news. The answer is unbelievably simple: Just ask. Just believe. Just say yes. He wants to give Himself freely to our souls. (That's what love does: it gives itself.) We only have to accept that gift. (That's true of human love too!)

And when you do that, when you say yes to God, when you let God make love to your soul, then your soul will get pregnant with God's love, and that love will naturally flow out into love for your neighbors. And that will make you happy because love alone can free you from the shell of your ego.

We can't do this on our own. We are too weak and too selfish. But God wants to do it in us, and He *will* do it when we let Him. He will give us the power to forget ourselves and just love Him and His children. (He will usually do this gradually, subtly, gently, and freely, like the turning of the tide or the coming of the morning.) And in making other people happy, we will find that we are happier than we have ever been before. For we are then sharing the very life of God.

P.S. Nearly all the arguments in this chapter I got from St. Thomas Aquinas' *Summa Theologica*. St. Thomas, in turn, got many of them from previous philosophers: Socrates, Plato, Aristotle, Augustine, and Boethius.

XV

Why is there evil?

1. Why is that *problem in this book?*

Because it is the most serious problem in the world.
This is so for three reasons.

First, evil is anti-God. It is the only anti-God thing in the world. God made the whole world and declared it good (Gen 1:31). But God did not make evil.

Second, evil is the only strong argument against the existence of God, the only reason for atheism: if God is good, why does He allow evil? There are dozens of arguments for the existence of God. We looked at ten of them in a previous chapter in this book. But evil is the *only* argument for atheism.

Third, evil is not only a problem of thought, an argument, but a problem of life. It affects us. It hurts us. It harms those we love. That's what evil is: something that harms people.

Life is full of good things. Some of them are very, very good things. But life is also full of very bad things: sin, suffering, and stupidity; disease, death, and disappointments; fears, follies, and failures. A religion that does not take account of the "dark side" of life is unrealistic and incomplete. The Catholic Church, like God Himself, has always taken evil seriously, in real life as well as in thought.

2. What is the Church's answer to evil?

The Church's answer to the problem of evil is Jesus Christ.

There are two problems of evil: in thought and in life. The problem of evil in thought is an argument, the argument for atheism: the reality of evil seems to prove the unreality of God. If God was real, He would wipe out all evil. But evil exists. Therefore, God is not real.

That is an important argument, and it has to be answered, and we will answer it in a little while. But the most important problem of evil is not the thought-problem but the life-problem. When you are sick, your main problem is not just solving the problem of sickness in thought, but in life, not just understanding why you were sick and how you got sick, but being cured.

Jesus has solved the problem of evil *there*, where it hurts most: not just in thought but in life. He did this not just by teaching about evil but by actually *entering into* evil, on the Cross, by suffering the worst of evils from the worst of people and by using that suffering and death to transform the meaning of suffering and death, to make the evils of suffering and death work for good, for our salvation. Christ made His *suffering* of evil part of our *salvation* from evil.

That is the Church's answer to the problem of evil. The Church gives us Jesus' answer to the problem of evil. And Jesus' answer to the problem of evil is Jesus. Not just the *teachings* of Jesus, but *Jesus*; not just "This is My mind" but "This is My Body." And He did not say, "Take and understand" but "Take and eat."

3. What is the solution to the problem of evil in thought?

Everyone has to deal with evil in *practice*. It's part of our world. But Christians also have to deal with the additional problem of evil in *thought*: evil seems to disprove God. If you don't believe in God, you can just say "evil happens" and leave it at that. If there is no God, there is no contradiction between evil and God. But if God is real, and evil is also real, there is apparently a contradiction between God and evil.

The problem is this: If God is all-good, He wants only good; and if He is all-powerful, He gets everything He wants. So why is there still evil? It seems that it must be either because God is not all-good or because He is not all-powerful.

Part of the answer to this question is that *we* made evil, not God. We freely chose it. God created our free will, but He did not create evil.

Another part of the answer is that God brings good even out of evil, but He does it gradually. We are in a story, not in an instant formula or equation. The story is called human history. History is really "His-story". But we haven't gotten yet to the part where they all live happily ever after.

Another part of the answer is that God brings good out of evil not against our will but with our will, by using our free choices of good as His instruments, by using us as His instruments, His warriors, His soldiers of love.

4. What is evil?

That is the question we need to start with. For we need clear definitions of our terms; otherwise, we will just be confused and get nowhere.

Evil is not a thing, an entity, a being, a substance. We can *imagine* it that way: as a dark cloud; or a Darth Vader; or a second God, a bad one. But that is not what evil is. It is not a *thing*, not a *being*. For God is totally good, and all things, all beings that God created are good. And no one else can create new beings. Only God can do that. So the only two kinds of beings, the Creator and the creatures (created beings), are both good—good in their being. All beings are good.

Even when one of these good creatures uses its free will to disobey God's will—for instance, when Cain murders Abel— that creature is still a good *being*, but it is choosing to do an evil *deed*, making an evil *choice*. It's a good creature, created by God, who is killing another good creature. And to do the evil deed, the killer has to use the good things God created in him, his mind and his will and his body. And he normally has to use one of the good things God created outside of him: for instance, a rock. It even has to be a "good" stroke of the rock to crush Abel's skull. In other words, all *moral* evil, all sin, has to use *physical* goods, like brains and arms and rocks.

Not all desires, choices, and deeds are good. Some are evil. But all *beings* are good. Cain's act of murdering Abel was an evil deed only because it harmed Abel's good being, Abel's human nature. And Cain had that same human nature.

Evil is the choice of the wrong order between good things: for instance, Cain's choice to put a rock on Abel's head instead of putting a kiss on Abel's head and a rock on the head of a rattlesnake. God created Cain and Abel and rocks and rattlesnakes, and all of them are good, even though some of them can be dangerous. Rocks and rattlesnakes can be dangerous for people for physical reasons: both can kill you. But other people are not supposed to be dangerous for people: they're not supposed to kill you but love you and help you. Evil is in our choices, not in God's creatures. Evil is our creation, not God's. That's true of moral evil, or sin, which is the worst kind of evil. But there is a second kind of evil, physical evil: disease and death and suffering. All moral evil is made by us, but most physical evil is not. We didn't make hurricanes and rattlesnakes and cancers. Moral evil comes from us, but physical evil comes *to* us. Moral evil is evil we do, but physical evil is evil we suffer. Moral evil is something we will to be, but physical evil is something we will *not* to be. Moral evils happen by our will, our bad choices, but physical evils happen against our will.

5. *So where did physical evils come from? Did God make them? Did He make rattlesnakes and hurricanes? Did He make diseases and death?*

God made rattlesnakes and hurricanes, and these things are dangerous, but they are not evil. They are things, and things are not evil.

But human suffering and death are evil. They do *not* come from God. "God did not make death" (Wis 1:13). God made us to live forever. He did not design us to suffer and die like animals. That fate we brought upon ourselves when we sinned.

He warned us against this. Genesis 3 is the story of how the two evils came into our life and how physical evil came because of moral evil. It shows the causal connection between the two kinds of evil.

It is a true story, a story of events that really happened in this world. But it is told in a symbolic way. Sin is symbolized as a forbidden fruit, and temptation is symbolized as a talking snake. These symbols are probably not meant to be taken literally, but they *are* meant to be taken seriously. The fall into sin really happened. If it didn't, then the good God created us sinful, and our sin is His fault, not ours.

To see the connection between moral evil and physical evil, between sin and suffering and death, think of a magnet with three iron rings attached to it. The magnet symbolizes God, and the three rings symbolize the soul, the body, and the material world. As long as the soul stays attached to God, the magnetism flows into the whole chain and the whole chain stays together. That chain symbolizes life before the Fall: the soul perfectly aligned with God in innocence, the body perfectly aligned with the soul in immortality, and the world perfectly aligned with the body in a pleasure garden of Eden. The magnetism symbolizes life: divine life in the magnet, spiritual life in the soul, biological life in the body, and daily life in the world.

Now imagine the first iron ring deciding to pull itself apart from the magnet. That symbolizes sin, asserting our own will against God. The result? The whole chain ceases to be magnetized. There's not enough magnetism (life) left in the first iron ring to keep the second one attached for long, so the second ring soon falls away. That symbolizes death: the separation of the body from the soul. And the world is no longer aligned with the body either. That symbolizes pain.

The point is that there is a causal connection between the two kinds of evils. Spiritual evil, or sin, is the ultimate cause of physical evil, or pain. Pain came into human life only after sin did. That's what the Genesis story tells us, under the form of the symbols of the two trees, a forbidden fruit, and a serpent. I have tried to explain it by another symbol: the magnet and the three iron rings.

The connection between sin and suffering explains why the

human race suffers pain, disease, and death. It does not explain why one individual suffers more pain than another. It certainly does not mean that the more pain you have, the more you are being punished for your sins. It does not tell you why *you* suffer but why *we* suffer. It tells us that it is sin that brought suffering into human life.

Until they sinned, our first parents experienced only the joy of living in God's presence.

Another way of seeing the connection between sin and suffering is to remember the connection between the soul and the body. They are not two different things. They are not even two connected things, like two iron rings. That is where my symbol is misleading. For the soul and the body are two inseparable *dimensions* of one and the same person, as the meaning of a book and the words of a book are two dimensions of the book. You can't help or harm one dimension of a human being without helping or harming the other dimension too, just as you can't change the words of a book without changing the meaning, and you can't change the meaning of a book without changing the words. We are not two things, angels plus animals, or spirits plus bodies, or ghosts trapped in machines; we are single persons with a spiritual dimension and a physical dimension. Whatever affects one dimension also affects the other. The soul that sins and the body that suffers are not two beings but two dimensions of the same being, man.

6. Is that why sin is so bad? Because it brought suffering into the world?

That's only part of it, and not the worst part. Sin is worse than suffering. Even if sin did not bring pain, it would be the worst of evils. Here are seven reasons why.

a. When we sin, we do it with our free will. Our free will is God's gift of a little of His own power, so to speak. Free will is part of the "image of God" in us. Only God, angels, and humans—that is, only *persons*—have free will. So when we sin we are misusing a holy thing. We are turning a godly thing, a thing from God, against God.

b. Here is another reason sin is so bad: because of our sins, God Himself had to suffer and die to save us. The price God paid for our sins was infinite.

c. Most sins come from human weakness, whether individual (of the "flesh") or social (of the "world"). But the one who is behind both the world and the flesh is the Devil. He uses the world and the flesh to tempt us, but all sin can be traced back to the Devil.

(By the way, the "flesh" means not just the body but the soul too, including our fallen thoughts, imaginations, desires, fears, and bad habits. And the "world" means all the bad influences on us from our fallen human society. The "world" does not mean the planet earth, the natural world, which is good, but it means the human world, fallen human culture.)

Jesus clearly taught us that the Devil is real. In fact, Jesus performed exorcisms. He cast out devils. He didn't just teach about the Devil—He *met* the Devil and overcame him.

d. If nothing is done about sin, if it is not redeemed or if we do not accept Christ's redemption, then eventually, when there is no more time left for change, it results in our eternal separation from God and from everything that is good. That is what Hell means. That too is the clear teaching of Jesus Himself. If Hell does not exist, Jesus is a fool or a liar. If Hell is not Hell, then Jesus is not Jesus.

e. If we are Christ's Body, we make *Christ's* Body to do whatever we do! That's what the Bible says (1 Cor 6:15).

f. When we harm others, we harm God's children. And when you harm the child, you harm the loving parent even more. Jesus says, "Whatever you do to one of the least of these, My brothers, you do to Me."

g. Every evil has a kick-back effect: every time we harm another person, we also harm ourselves. We turn ourselves into something a little more evil.

So there are no fewer than seven reasons why sin is so terrible.

7. *Isn't it terribly negative, dark, and pessimistic to take evil so seriously? Isn't the Church hung up on the negative, on nonos? Doesn't this make us unhappy and guilty and take away our smiles? Isn't Christianity supposed to be the "Gospel", or the "good news" that God loves us?*

Christianity is the "good news" indeed, but this good news makes no sense unless you believe the bad news first. The good news is like the offer of a free heart transplant operation from God; but if you don't think your heart is desperately diseased, you won't see that offer as good news at all. As Jesus said, "Those who are well have no need of a physician, but those who are sick; I came not to call the righteous, but sinners" (Mk 2:17). He said this to the Pharisees, the self-righteous fools who thought they were just good people who didn't need to repent of sin. The good news of forgiveness is really good news only because the bad news of sin is really bad news. The greater the problem, the greater the solution. The deeper the valley, the higher the mountain.

Jesus Himself tell us the bad news of sin as well as the good news of salvation. The Church just repeats His message. You can't find out whether this message is true by looking at your feelings. Of course negative ideas like sin and evil and punishment and Hell and demons are going to make you have negative feelings. If they don't, there's something wrong with you! Cancers and wars and starvation also give you bad feelings. But they're real, and you have to deal with them. The question is: What is real? Are these evils real or not? The Church says they are because she says what Christ said. Do we judge our feelings by Christ, or do we judge Christ by our feelings? Are our feelings the divine, infallible, perfect Word of God? Or is that Jesus?

The question is not *about* feelings but about facts. The question is not about psychology but about reality.

Jesus, the Bible, and the Church give us a picture of human life as a spiritual war with Christ on one side and evil on the other side. This picture is not a bitter, dark pessimism. Neither is it a naïve, easy, breezy optimism. It is realism. "Realism" means simply living in reality, not fantasy, taking account of everything real.

Evil is real. And good is real. And good is stronger than evil. Those are tremendous truths. And only one of the three truths is dark. Light and darkness are not equal.

Christianity is war, but it is a spiritual war. "For we are not contending against flesh and blood, but against the principalities, against the powers, against the world rulers of this present darkness, against the spiritual hosts of wickedness in the heavenly places" (Eph 6:12). We should take our enemy very seriously, for "the Devil prowls around like a roaring lion, seeking some one to devour" (1 Pet 5:8). But we should also be absolutely confident of victory. Jesus told us both of these two truths, the bad news and the good news, when He said, "In the world you have tribulation; but be of good cheer, I have overcome the world" (Jn 16:33). Tyrants try to conquer the world by power and always fail. Jesus is conquering the world by love and is succeeding.

For there is no force in the universe stronger than the love of God. "Who shall separate us from the love of Christ? Shall tribulation, or distress, or persecution, or famine, or nakedness, or peril, or sword? As it is written, 'For thy sake we are being killed all the day long; we are regarded as sheep to be slaughtered.' No, in all these things we are more than conquerors through him who loved us. For I am sure that neither death, nor life, nor angels, nor principalities, nor things present, nor things to come, nor powers, nor height, nor depth, nor anything else in all creation, will be able to separate us from the love of God in Christ Jesus our Lord" (Rom 8:35–39).

The good news that "God so loved the world that he gave his only Son that whoever believes in him should not perish but have eternal life" (Jn 3:16) is such incredibly good news that it sounds too good to be true. "There is no tale ever told that man would more want to be true", says Tolkien. And the best news of all is that it *is*.

8. How does evil fit into the "good news"?

To see this, let's first review why we call it "good news".

Christianity is news. It is a story, a true story, a history, a narrative. The Bible is a book of events, from the Creation to the Last Judgment. And in the middle of the story is the most important event that ever happened, the "Jesus-event", the Incarnation of God into time and history, the birth and life and death and Resurrection of the Savior. That is God's answer to evil. It is like a D-day invasion of the world after the Devil had corrupted it. It is a drama. It is the most dramatic story in the world. It is not just a set of abstract, eternal principles of theology and morality. That is only its road map.

9. Who is Jesus in this story?

Jesus is not only the teacher who has the answer to the problem of evil; He *is* the answer. He is the live-action hero of the drama. He doesn't just solve the puzzle of why there is evil—He *destroys* evil, He conquers Satan, He frees His children (us) from Satan's captivity. That's why He went to the Cross.

All the heroes in all the stories in the world are heroes only because they are in some ways like Jesus: Antigone, Beatrice, Frodo Baggins, Ulysses, Oedipus, Billy Budd, Alyosha Karamazov, Socrates, King Arthur, Beowulf, Roland, Aeneas, Luke Skywalker, Peter Pevensie, and millions of mothers throughout history.

10. If Jesus is the hero who solves the problem of evil, then what must we do to solve the problem of evil?

First, we must believe in Him, trust in Him, love Him, and adore Him as our hero, our Savior, and our Lord.

Second, we must be like Jesus. We must grow into Him (Eph 4:13). For He showed us not only what perfect divinity is but also what we are, what perfect humanity is, what we must all become.

Like Jesus, we must not only answer the argument about evil, but we must take up the actual fight against it. We must be not only His students but His disciples, His friends, His followers, His children, His family, His army. We must do His work of fighting evil by using His weapons of love and truth, mercy and justice, charity and courage, joy and suffering, life and death. For He left *us*, the Church, to finish His work.

Third, we must be like Jesus not just by *imitating* Him but by becoming *incorporated* into Him, into His Body, by getting "plugged into" His very life. That is what happens when we eat His Body and drink His Blood in Holy Communion. The very same lifeblood that flows through Christ then flows through us, as the very same sap that flows through the tree flows through its branches. That is what Jesus Himself said to His disciples: "I am the vine, you are the branches" (Jn 15:5).

XVI

Why must we die?

All the religions of the world deal with the same questions, the same problems, and the same mysteries, though they give different answers to them. Some of those questions concern death: Why must we die? What happens after death? What can we do to prepare for it?

The Church summarizes her answers in her doctrine of the Four Last Things: death, judgment, Heaven, and Hell.

1. Isn't the question of death, and life after death, impractical for young people? Isn't it escapism to think about life after death? Doesn't it take away your attention and care for this world?

No. It is very practical for young people to think about death, because young people die too sometimes. And we will all die, eventually. *When* you will die is life's great uncertainty, but *whether* you will die is life's great certainty.

We need to think about the biggest things in life, and death is one of the very biggest things in life. People who see friends or family members die almost always say the same thing: even when the death is expected, they are deeply moved. The event was different from other events. It was *big*. As big as the sky. For when a loved one dies, it does not feel like a *part* of the world has died, even a large part; it feels like the *whole* world has died. The death of a parent, especially, or a spouse, is, in C. S. Lewis' words, "like the sky: spread over everything".

It's not escapism to think about life after death either. It's realism. The next world is not a fantasy, like *Star Wars*. It's real, like New York. In fact, it's escapism *not* to think about it. For we are all already on this journey.

Imagine you are on a plane headed to another country, with a one-way ticket. You don't know how long it will take you to leave your present country, but you know that when you do, you will never return. Is it escapism to prepare for the journey? Is it escapism to think about the country you are headed to? Is it escapism to be sure you are on the right plane?

The saints prove by their lives that it is not escapism to believe in the next world. Those who have believed most strongly in the next world have always done the most for this world. Believing that this world leads to the next makes you think of this world *more* carefully. It makes this world *more* precious. When a woman is pregnant, she takes special care of her body, so that her baby is born healthy. This world is like a pregnant woman: if you believe that you are going to be born out of this world into another, bigger world, you will take more care of this world, not less. The roads that led to the gold mines in California in 1849 were well taken care of because they led to an important place, while the roads that led to ghost towns in the desert were not taken care of but neglected. If you believe this world is a road to Heaven, you will care for it more, not less, than if you believe it is a dead end.

2. *How do we know there is life after death at all? Maybe it's just a myth. There's no proof of it. Nobody ever came back to tell us about it.*

Not true. Somebody did come back to tell us about it. His name is Jesus. He died and rose from the dead. If that's not true, our whole religion is a lie.

Many ordinary people have also caught glimpses of the next world in near-death experiences. Millions of people, in fact. They were not all dreaming or hallucinating or making it up. They were certain. They *saw* it.

And there are good logical arguments for life after death too. Some people don't need these arguments; they "just know", intuitively, innately. But other people have doubts, consciously or unconsciously, and sometimes these doubts are serious worries. Good arguments can strengthen your faith if it is weak and full of doubts. And even if you don't personally need these proofs, it's good to know them so that you can give them to other people who do need them because they do have doubts. (These arguments are like the arguments for the existence of God in that way.)

Here are six arguments for life after death.

a. *The argument from authority.* This is not a proof but it is a strong clue. The vast majority of all people who have ever lived, in all nations, cultures, races, and religions, have believed in life after death. Most of the people who deny it are confined to one or two centuries (the most recent centuries) and one civilization (our own modern Western post-Christian materialistic civilization). And even there, such people are a small minority. The vast majority of the sages, or wise men, have taught it through the centuries. All the religions of the world teach some form of it. And above all, Jesus clearly taught it. If all these people are wrong, then you have to be a snob, for only you and your very small circle of unbelievers are right while the rest of the human race, including the best and wisest people who have ever lived, have all been wrong about this crucial question. How likely is that?

We innately believe in life after death. Children have to be conditioned out of it, not into it. It is natural. That does not prove it is true, but it is certainly a clue. You have to distrust human nature a lot to ignore this clue.

b. *The argument from desire.* The desire to conquer death is in all of us. We all find death scandalous. The desire for immortality is natural and universal (in all of us).

Every single one of our other desires that are natural and universal correspond to real things that can satisfy them. There is hunger—and there is food. There is thirst—and there is drink. There is loneliness—and there is society. There is curiosity—and there is knowledge. There is sexual desire—and there is sex. There is tiredness—and there is sleep. There is the desire for beauty—and there is beauty. And there is the desire for life after death—and there is no such thing? Why should this one innate and universal desire, the deepest one of all, be the only exception? If there is no immortality, why do we naturally desire it? If a duck longs for water, it was designed to swim.

c. *The argument from the soul not having parts.* We are not just bodies; we are also souls. The soul is the source of life to the body. When the body loses its life, it does not lose any atoms, but it loses *something.* Something in us is not composed of atoms.

When we die, we fall apart into body-without-a-soul and soul-without-a-body. And then the body falls apart into organs, which no longer work together, and the organs into tissues, and the tissues into cells, and the cells into molecules. Everything that has parts can fall apart. But the soul has no parts. You don't have half a soul. You might have a weak soul, or a bad soul, or a stupid soul, but you never have a tenth of a soul. You don't lose any part of your soul when you lose part of your hair or fingernails, or even a limb.

A sword or a bullet or a cancer can split apart a body and

kill it. But no sword or bullet or cancer can kill a soul because nothing can split the soul into pieces. It has no pieces.

So none of the things that can kill the body can kill the soul.

d. *The argument from reason and free will.* (This argument will probably be harder to follow than the others, so don't worry if you don't understand it all. But I put it in because it's good to have a challenge that stretches your mind now and then and also because it's a very important point about human nature, about who you are, and about how you are different from an animal. Many people are confused about this point today, and it's important that you are not confused about it.)

Our souls can perform two acts that are spiritual, not just physical; therefore, our souls must be spiritual. And what is spiritual is not mortal. Therefore our souls are immortal.

We can know abstract eternal truths like "Justice is a virtue" or "$2 + 2 = 4$", and we can freely choose between right and wrong. Animals cannot do those two things because they do not have spiritual souls. They have biological life, unlike rocks, and they have feelings, unlike plants—even some surprisingly human feelings like affection—and they have very clever instincts. But they don't have reason or free will. Human thinking is rational understanding, and human choosing is free and morally responsible. Human thinking is not just sensation and imagination, and human willing is not just feeling and instinct. Put reason and free choice together and you get morality. Morality presupposes these two things: understanding right and wrong, and freely choosing between right and wrong.

That is why we don't just *train* humans, as we train dogs, and why we don't preach to dogs, as we preach to humans. When the dog pees on the carpet, we don't tell him to go to confession! And when we sin, we don't just whine and slink away from our master. We repent and go *to* our Master.

You can observe in yourself your power to do these two things that animals cannot do. First of all, take your ability to think rationally, beyond sensation and sensory imagination. You can both see and imagine the difference between a three-sided figure and a four-sided figure, and animals can too. But if you take a course in geometry, you can also *understand* that difference. And you can understand things you cannot imagine. You cannot imagine the difference between a thirty-three-sided figure and a thirty-four-sided figure, but you can understand it and calculate it. You can *imagine* the difference between a man and a woman, but you cannot imagine the difference between a just man and an unjust man. But you can understand it.

You can also observe in yourself the second thing that raises you above animals: the difference between free will and animal instinct. When you see something flying through the air at your face, you close your eyes instinctively, just as an animal does. But when you see something you think you shouldn't see, like the answers on the test paper of the classmate in front of you, you close your eyes deliberately and by free choice. Or else you look deliberately. You can choose to look or not to look, to cheat or not to cheat.

A spiritual act can come only from a spiritual actor. A spiritual effect can come only from a spiritual cause. Rational thinking and free moral choosing are spiritual acts, so they must come from a spiritual cause—from a soul, not merely a body. ("Spiritual" here means not-physical, not-material. It doesn't mean *religious*.)

Of course the soul is *dependent on* the body. It uses the body as an instrument. It uses the body's brain as you use your computer. When your computer crashes, you can't use it, and when your brain is damaged, you can't think.

But the brain is not the soul any more than your computer is you.

However, the relation between the soul and the brain is not the same as the relation between you and your computer. The soul is the very life of the body and of the brain that is one of the body's organs. You are not the very life of your computer.

e. *The argument from God.* If there is no life after death, there is no God, and you have to be an atheist. For if God exists, then immortality must exist also because of divine justice. Not everyone gets what they deserve in this life, and if there is no next life, then there is no justice in the end; and if justice does not have the last word, then a God of justice does not exist.

Also, if God exists, then immortality exists because of God's love. If you love someone, you want him to live. If even we selfish human beings want those people we love to live, how much more must God want this? Does God love your dear departed family member less than you do?

f. *The argument from the intrinsic value of the person.* (This is another "stretch" argument and another very important one because it's about what kind of value you have as a person.)

If death is the end, and there is no life after death, then people are treated like cars. You can replace your car, but you can't replace your friend. If reality treats people like cars, then reality is immoral. And if reality is immoral, why take morality seriously? If the deepest moral values—the intrinsic value of persons—has no ground in reality; if this idea that persons are intrinsically valuable and ought to be loved as ends rather than used as means—if this idea is only our subjective feeling or desire, then there is no objectively real obligation to love people, to treat them as ends and as unique and irreplace-able.

But you can understand this argument only if you love. Love opens your eyes. When you love someone, you get new eyes: you see something you never saw before. You see that the person you love has intrinsic value, unique value, irreplaceable value, absolute value rather than relative value. You see that this person—and every person—is not a means but an end. Pope John Paul II loved to quote this saying of the documents of Vatican II: "Man is the only creature in the universe that God willed for his own sake." Love gives you Godlike eyes. You *see* this as a basic truth of morality: that we ought to love people, not use them, and to use things, not love them. And once you see that, the argument follows. Once you see people's value, you see their immortality.

These six arguments are only a sample. There are many more arguments for believing in life after death, just as there are many more arguments for the existence of God. For instance, you can apply Pascal's wager to the question of eternal life: even if you can't prove immortality, you can't disprove it either. And what can you gain by disbelieving it? Nothing. But what can you gain by believing it? Everything.

3. *What is the Last Judgment? When we die, will we meet God as just Judge or as loving Savior?*

Both! We know that because He told us. Christianity is not a do-it-yourself, figure-it-out-for-yourself religion. The Church just delivers the mail she received from Christ. She didn't write the mail, and she stubbornly refuses to be so arrogant as to edit and correct God's mail, to add to it or subtract from it.

That's what heretics do. (We call them "dissenters" now. It's more polite.)

God must judge everyone because God is truth, God is light, God is justice. You cannot hide from God.

This, by the way, is also what all the people who have had a near-death experience say: they meet a "being of light", and nothing can be hidden from this light. Everything is known, everything comes out into the light of truth, everything is judged justly and truly. They also say that this being of light is absolute love as well as absolute truth. They knew they were *loved* totally and absolutely as well as *known* totally and absolutely. Neither love nor truth, neither mercy nor justice, can be compromised.

God reconciled justice and mercy, justice and love, in Christ on the Cross. Christ got the justice, and we got the mercy.

But justice must be done. There's no free lunch. Nobody gets away with anything with God. Every evil *must* be punished, just as every good *must* be rewarded.

God forgives, yes. In fact, God forgives *all* our sins. But the price for sin still has to be paid. If I forgive you your debt of $1,000 to me, you do not have to pay it. But I do! God forgave us our debt because He paid it Himself, on the Cross.

God is like the judge in court whose daughter was on trial for reckless driving. The law required a $10,000 fine. The judge found his daughter guilty and fined her $10,000. Then he stepped down from the bench and took out his checkbook and paid the fine himself out of his own money.

In God, justice and love are one thing, not two things. Justice is the form His love takes. Justice is not the opposite of love; justice is "tough love".

What does God judge at the Last Judgment? First and most important, God judges whether we go to Heaven or Hell. How does He combine justice and mercy here? If we have His life in us, if we have allowed Him to enter our souls by faith, hope, and charity, we will go to Heaven. Not because we deserve it, but because we can endure it. No one can buy Heaven with enough good deeds. (How many would be enough?) It is God's free gift of grace. Faith is our acceptance of that gift. Those who do not accept that gift do not have it. Those who reject God do not have His life in them, and they would not be able to enjoy Heaven even if they were put there, because what Heaven is made of is truth and justice and holiness and un-selfish love—that is what God is "made of"—and that is what they have rejected. They would hate Heaven, as deeply evil people hate goodness.

That is the first thing God judges: who goes to Heaven. Jesus spoke of that in His parable of the sheep and the goats in Matthew 25:32–33.

The second thing God judges is whether we need Purga-tory before Heaven, whether we need purgation—that is, pu-rifying, preparation, or cleansing of our souls—before we can enter Heaven and endure its light and goodness. Most of us probably do. If we need that cleansing, we will go to Purgatory first, and then to Heaven after we are purged of all selfishness and bad habits and character faults. (See question 8, on Pur-gatory.)

The third thing God judges is how *much* of Heaven we can endure. We will not all be equal in Heaven, though we will all be equally loved by God. He loves each of us totally, but a great saint can receive more of that love and reflect more of it back. A big mirror can reflect more of the sun's light than a small one, even though the sun gives all of its light out and does not keep anything back. A quart milk carton and a half-gallon milk carton can both be totally full of milk—the same milk—

yet there is twice as much milk in one as in the other. Every soul in Heaven will be totally full of God's joy and truth, but some will be able to contain more of it than others. But all will be fully content, because there is no envy in Heaven, only in Hell. (Envy makes you miserable, and there is no misery in Heaven.)

The meaning of life is to make yourself—or rather, to let God make you—into a bigger bottle, a bigger mirror, a bigger soul, a more generous soul, a bigger person, a more loving person forever. Love has eternal consequences.

4. Many people believe in reincarnation. They believe their souls will come back to earth in other bodies. Is that possible?

No.

First of all, the Bible clearly teaches that reincarnation is not true: "It is appointed for men to die once, and after that comes judgment" (Heb 9:27).

Second, it is not possible because the body is as much a part of your unique individual personality as your soul. Those who believe in reincarnation always believe that the body is only a thing like a motel room or a suit of clothes that you can move in and out of. They also do not believe in the resurrection of the body (of each individual body) at the end of the world, which the Bible and the Church teach as truth. In fact, the "resurrection of the body" is one of the twelve articles (points) of the Church's first and oldest creed, the Apostles' Creed.

People often believe in reincarnation for a very good reason: they sense that they are not finished yet when they die. They are right about that, but that's why there is Purgatory. Most of us have to be finished (perfected, purified, purged) before we can enter Heaven. But God does that to us in Purgatory; we don't do it ourselves by coming back and living more lives on earth.

Belief in reincarnation tends to have a very bad effect on your attitude toward life in this world. If you believe in reincarnation, you do not think that any one lifetime on earth is terribly important. So you can easily think that you can waste your life and sin all you want, because you will always get a second chance in your next reincarnation. It is like believing that it doesn't matter whether you pass or fail an exam because if you fail it you can always try again tomorrow, and the next day, and forever, until you pass it; that there is no such thing as a *final* exam. That takes all the drama out of life, and all the danger. If you don't "go around only once in life", you don't live life with gusto.

But if each life is a matter of life or death, if each life is final and not repeatable, then each individual is also not repeatable. The infinite preciousness of life and the infinite preciousness of each individual go together, and belief in reincarnation weakens both. It is deeply insulting if you say to someone you love that he is not absolutely unique, that he once was somebody else, long ago, and will be somebody else again after he dies. That is not what love says. Love sees in the beloved's life something absolutely unique and irreplaceable.

5. *Are we really supposed to believe in a literal Heaven, with golden streets and fluffy white clouds and angels playing harps?*

That's like asking whether you're really supposed to believe there is an island made of a large green jewel hundreds of miles wide when you are told that Ireland, the "Emerald Isle", really exists. Ireland does really exist, and it really is very green, *like* emeralds, but it is not made of a literal emerald. That is an image, a symbol, not to be taken literally. Similarly, Heaven really exists, but the imagery for the things in Heaven is not to be taken literally.

The popular images of golden streets, fluffy clouds, haloes, and angel harps are not even in the Bible. Other images of Heaven *are* found in the Bible: an enormous city with twelve gates, a wedding feast, thrones, a crystal sea, and so forth. These are images God has revealed, and therefore they are to be believed, but believed as imagery. They are not to be taken literally. Symbols are to be taken symbolically. We know the images are not meant to be interpreted literally because the Bible describes Heaven in these words: "What no eye has seen, nor ear heard, nor the heart of man conceived, what God has prepared for those who love him" (1 Cor 2:9).

For instance, Heaven is described as a wedding feast (Rev 21:2; 22:17), but this is not a literal wedding because Jesus says that in Heaven "they neither marry nor are given in marriage" (Mt 22:30). In Heaven there are no new babies, no gradual growing up from infancy to old age, and no private families to bring new children into the world and nourish them; therefore, there are no weddings or marriages. So the heavenly wedding is symbolic. It means the spiritual marriage, the spiritual union, the spiritual love between God and man, between Christ and His Church, His Body, His people (us!). It is like a marriage because marriage is the most intimate and total love relationship possible on earth. Or rather, a marriage on earth is like *it*. Heaven is more, not less, than any earthly image can say.

Similarly, the imagery for Hell is not to be taken literally. The fire is not physical fire from this world. But the symbolic

interpretation is stronger, not weaker, than the literal inter-
pretation. For Hell's "fire" destroys not just bodies but souls
(Mt 10:28). Just as Heaven is far better than we can imagine,
Hell is far worse.

6. *What will be in Heaven? Beer? Baseball? Catbirds? Cats?*

Obviously, we don't know, any more than an unborn baby
knows what's in the world outside the womb. What we do
know is what God has told us: that He loves us and has "prepared a place" for us (Jn 14:1–3; Mt 25:34; Heb 1:16). It is
a place *for us*. We know this much, then: we will not feel for-
gotten or foreign or fearful but will feel *at home*. And we will
be perfectly happy. "He will wipe away every tear from their
eyes" (Rev 21:4). So *if* we need beer, or baseball, or catbirds,
or cats for our complete happiness, then they will be there.
God can do anything. "With God all things are possible" (Mt
19:26).

We know that we will have resurrected bodies in Heaven,
immortal bodies like the body of Jesus after His Resurrection.
Since we will have bodies, we will live in a bodily world, which
the Bible calls "a new heaven [sky] and a new earth" (Rev 21:1;
2 Pet 3:13). We will not be turned into angels, which are pure
spirits. And other living things, plants and animals or something like plants and animals, will probably also be there. For
God designed Heaven *for us*, remember. We are humans, and
our humanity will be perfected, not set aside. A world without
plants and animals seems hardly fit for human habitation. So
even though the soul of your cat is not immortal, as your soul
is, God may well bring your cat to life in Heaven to be with
you. He certainly *can* do that.

Make a list of all the things you really love. Everything in the list, and much more, will be in Heaven, though in some new, surprising, transformed, perfected form.

But the most important thing about Heaven is not *what* will be in Heaven but *who*; not the things but the people. Even on earth, things do not make us deeply happy or unhappy; only people can do that.

So who will be in Heaven? Everyone who chooses to be, everyone who wants to be, everyone who loves what Heaven is and what God is, namely truth and love, honesty and unselfishness. (See Rev 22:17.)

And these people will relate to each other in Heaven in total truth and light and honesty, in total love and acceptance and forgiveness. For that is what the life of Heaven will be full of, because that is what God's life is full of. That is why even on earth these two heavenly things are the two things that make us the most deeply happy: truth and love. And they are also the two things that do not ever get boring: knowing and loving.

The persons in Heaven will include not only human beings but also angels, the pure spirits God created. They are non-human persons, persons without human bodies. They too are persons because they too can say "I", as God can. (When God revealed His own name, that is the word He used: "I AM" [Ex 3:14].) The angels also can know and love God, each other, and us.

In fact, the angels—especially our guardian angels—know and love us now. God has appointed a guardian angel invisibly to guard and guide each individual through that person's entire life. (Jesus told us that in Matthew 18:20.) When you get to Heaven, you will meet and thank your angel.

Most important of all, in Heaven we will know and be known

by God, and we will love and be loved by God. Deep down, that is what we all desire above all, even though we may not think we do. We can't imagine this because we can't imagine God, and it's hard for us to desire what we can't imagine. Yet our hearts are deeper than our imaginations, and our hearts are restless until they rest in Him because He designed our hearts that way. We were designed to be unable to find perfect, total happiness in this world, even if we possess the whole world. Each single human heart is bigger than the whole world. We long for infinite truth, infinite goodness (love), and infinite beauty, and we are not totally satisfied with anything less. And only God is infinite truth, infinite goodness, and infinite beauty.

7. *Is there really a Hell? Isn't that belief primitive, crude, and cruel? Isn't it just a popular myth?*

No, it isn't. In fact, it's only a popular myth that Hell *doesn't* exist. And it's also cruel *not to* believe in Hell. For isn't it cruel to tell skaters on thin ice that there's no water under the ice and that they can't possibly drown?

As Heaven is the object of our deepest desire, Hell is the object of our deepest fear. Our hearts are so deep that we don't even know our deepest desires and fears very clearly. But we do know that these two things match each other: our deepest desire is to be freed from our deepest fear, and our deepest fear is that we fail to attain our deepest desire. So if our deepest desire is to be in a love relationship with God—with infinite understanding, infinite love, and infinite beauty—then our deepest fear is to fail to attain that deepest desire forever, to have no hope of attaining it anymore. That's why in Dante's

Inferno the sign over the gate of Hell reads: "Abandon all hope, ye who enter here." As C. S. Lewis puts it in *The Problem of Pain*, "All your life an unattainable ecstasy has hovered just beyond the grasp of your consciousness. The day is coming when you will wake to find, beyond all hope, that you have attained it; or else, that it was within your reach and you have lost it forever."

If you understand who God is—infinite beauty, love, and truth—and if you understand who you are—a heart that needs this more than it needs anything else, even food and drink and air—then you will understand that it doesn't really matter whether or not there are physical fires and physical pains in Hell. For losing God means losing *everything*. And gaining God means gaining everything.

Hell must exist because if we have free will, then even though God loves us totally, we can still choose not to accept His love. God forgives us, but we can choose not to accept His forgiveness. Forgiveness is a free gift of God, but a free gift needs to be freely accepted as well as freely given. If we do not accept God's offer of free Heaven, we do not have it.

No one goes to Hell because God casts them into Hell, throws them in against their will. God is love; He does not throw us around like footballs. But that also means that He doesn't just throw us into Heaven like a football either. He respects our free choice.

8. Is Purgatory a little bit of Hell?

No, it's more like a little bit of Heaven. It's like Heaven's bathroom, where you go first to take a hot shower before you go to the banquet hall, because you look and smell like a tramp, full of dirt and scabs. The shower hurts, but you want it anyway, for you want to be clean. You *want* God to shape you up, to strip off the old snakeskin, to rip off the dirty bandages, to separate you totally from all your sinful habits. That will hurt. But it will also feel great.

The pains of Purgatory will be greater than the pains of earth, because you will see clearly, with no hiding, how ugly your sins were and how they harmed others and disappointed and dishonored God. But the joys of Purgatory will also be far greater than the joys of earth, for three reasons: (a) you will know that you are infallibly headed for Heaven, (b) you will not be able to sin anymore, and (c) God will be there with you, holding you by the hand as you "walk through the valley of the shadow of death", and you will fear no evil because He is with you. You will know that it is His perfect, divine love that is causing you your purgatorial pains, to free you from everything imperfect in you.

Therefore, you will want that purgation more than you have ever wanted anything in the world. You will freely will your Purgatory; you will say, "*Please* give me my Purgatory" as the tramp said, "Please let me take a hot shower before dinner."

We need Purgatory because God is a perfectionist. He loves us too much to settle for anything less than our very best. Jesus says that: "Be perfect, as your heavenly Father is perfect" (Mt 5:48).

If your teeth are too dirty for the dentist to fix, he will give you a cleaning first. If your body is dirty, your surgeon will insist you be washed before you can be operated on. If your parents come home from a sweaty, smelly soccer game and want to go out to dinner, they will take a shower first. That's why God justly and lovingly gives us Purgatory.

Most of us need Purgatory because we are not good enough to enjoy or endure Heaven without it, but we are not bad enough to go to Hell, with no hope for Heaven. Our faith, hope, and charity (the three glues that glue us to God) are real but weak. If they were not real, if they were not there at all, we would not have any hope of Heaven. If they were not weak, we would not need Purgatory.

We do not know whether Purgatory is an objective place, like Heaven, or whether it is just a state of mind, a state of soul, a process of change in our soul. If we get our resurrected bodies before Purgatory, then it must be an objective place. If we get our resurrected bodies after Purgatory, then Purgatory may be a state of mind, a cleansing of our memories and desires. It doesn't really matter much. What matters is that it is real, and God perfects our souls there so that we can be with Him in Heaven forever.

We also don't know whether Purgatory takes a literal, measurable time or not. When the Church tells us that a certain good deed (like a novena or a pilgrimage) will free us from "300 days in Purgatory" or "60 days in Purgatory", that language is to be taken symbolically, because Purgatory is not in this physical universe, so it cannot be measured by earthly clocks and by the passage of the sun through the sky. Perhaps Purgatory will be instantaneous, like ripping a bandage off a wound all at once; or perhaps it will take time even though that time cannot be measured by our material clocks. That too does not matter much. What matters is that it is real, and God perfects our souls there so that we can be with Him in Heaven forever.

9. *What difference does this all make to life here and now? How does this Catholic map of the future change the present? What difference does eternity make to Monday morning?*

It makes life infinitely dramatic. The stakes are eternal. Our choices are choices of different roads, and there is not one road that does not eventually lead to either Heaven or Hell, infinite bliss or infinite misery, unimaginable ecstasy or unimaginable failure, all or nothing. Heaven is the eternal presence of infinite joy, given to us by God, the source of all joy. Hell is the eternal absence of that, of all joy. The difference is total. The difference is infinite.

You can have infinite passion only about something that makes an infinite difference—ultimately, only about Heaven and Hell. That's why Jesus said such passionate things about Hell. For instance, He said, "If your eye causes you to sin, pluck it out and throw it from you; it is better for you to enter [eternal] life with one eye than with two eyes to be thrown into the hell of fire" (Mt 18:9). This sounds fanatical, but it is actually totally reasonable. "For what does it profit a man, to gain the whole world and forfeit his life [soul]?" (Mk 8:36). No man in the history of the world has ever uttered a more practical, more reasonable sentence than that one.

Life after death also makes an infinite difference in how we treat each other now, in this life. If we believe we are only clever apes with bigger brains who live for no more than a hundred years, then how will we treat each other? Like clever apes with bigger brains who live for no more than a hundred years! And then nations would be more important than individuals, for nations live much longer. But if we believe we are more like angels than apes; if we believe we are the kids of

King God, not the kids of King Kong; then we will treat each other that way: as infinitely precious and as infinitely more important than nations because when all nations are dead, each of us will still be alive. In fact, billions of years from now when the very stars have died, we will still be young.

10. How does Jesus fit into all this?

He Himself tells us the answer to that question: "I am the door" (Jn 10:9); "I am the resurrection and the life" (Jn 11:25); "I am the way, and the truth, and the life; no one comes to the Father but by me" (Jn 14:6).

This does not mean that only Christians can be saved. But it means that when anyone is saved, it is Christ who saves him.

Christ did not say, "Only Christians will be saved." Rather, He said, "*All* who seek, will find; all who knock, to them the door will be opened" (see Mt 7:7–8). There will probably be many good, God-seeking Muslims, Jews, Hindus, Buddhists, and even agnostics in Heaven. But when they get there, they will discover that it was Jesus who got them there.

Christians don't claim to be the only ones who are saved. But they do claim that Jesus is the only Savior—because Jesus Himself claimed that. It's not arrogant for us to claim that. It would be arrogant for us to deny it, because then we would be denying what Jesus told us, judging Jesus as wrong, setting ourselves up as His judge and claiming to correct His mistakes and exaggerations. If that's not arrogant, what is?

A Christian is one who has been given the incredible gift of knowing Christ. With greater knowledge comes greater responsibility. God does not give us knowledge just to satisfy our curiosity but for us to act on that knowledge. That is why we need the sacrament of Confirmation: to prepare us for adult action, adult life, adult faith, adult responsibilities. Adulthood is not a concept; it is real. And to succeed at it, we need to be confirmed (strengthened) with the God who is real, in fact is more real than anything else.

Conclusion

The answer to all sixteen questions is:

BECAUSE GOD IS REAL.